*Matoaks als Rebecka daughter to the mighty Prince
Powhatan Emperour of Attanougskomouck als virginia
converted and baptized in the Christian faith, and
wife to the worṭ Mr Joh Rolff*

From Weddell, *A Memorial Volume of Virginia Historical Portraiture*

THE FIRST SEVENTEEN YEARS
Virginia, 1607-1624

CHARLES E. HATCH, JR.

University Press of Virginia
Charlottesville and London

PRINTED IN THE UNITED STATES OF AMERICA

CONTENTS

FOREWORD

The colonization of Virginia was a mammoth undertaking even though launched by a daring and courageous people in an expanding age. The meager knowledge already accumulated was at hand to draw on and England was not without preparation to push for "its place in the sun." There was a growing navy, there was trained leadership, there was capital, there was organization and there were men ready to make the gamble for themselves and to the glory of God and for their country.

It remained for the Virginia Company of London, under its charter of April 10, 1606, to found the first permanent English settlement in America. This company, a commerical organization from its inception, assumed a national character, since its purpose was to "deduce" a "colony." It was instrumental, under its charter provisions, in guaranteeing to the settlers in the New World the rights, freedoms, and privileges enjoyed by Englishmen at home as well as the enjoyment of their customary manner of living which they adapted to their new environment with the passage of years. Quite naturally the settlers brought with them their church and reverence for God, maintained trial by jury and their rights as free men, and soon were developing representative government at Jamestown.

The immediate and long-range reasons for the settlement were many and, perhaps, thoroughly mixed. Profit and exploitation of the country were expected, for, after all, this was a business enterprise. A permanent settlement was the objective. Support, financial and popular, came from a cross section of English life. It seems obvious from accounts and papers of the period that it was generally thought that Virginia was being settled for the glory of God, for the honor of the King, for the welfare of England, and for the advancement of the Company and its individual members.

In England, and in Virginia, they expected and did carry the word of God to the natives, although not with the same verve as the Spanish. They expected to develop natural resources, to free the mother country from dependence on European states, to strengthen their navy, and to increase national wealth and power. They expected to be a thorn in the side of the Spanish Empire; in fact, they hoped one day to challenge and overshadow that empire. They sought to find the answer to what seemed to be unemployment at home. They sought many things not the least of them being gold, silver, land and personal advancement. As the men stepped ashore on Jamestown Island, perhaps each had a slightly different view of why he was there, yet some one or a combination of these motives was probably the reason.

The first section of this account is an adaptation, by the author of the booklet, *Jamestown, Virginia: The Town Site and Its Story* (National Park Service, Historical Handbook Series, No. 2) published by the Government Printing Office, Washington, D. C., 1949.

Portrait from John Smith's *General History* (London, 1624). Courtesy of
the Tracy W. McGregor Library, University of Virginia.

"James Fort" built in May and June, 1607—A painting by Sidney King for Colonial National Historical Park.

The Arrival of the Settlers at Jamestown on May 13, 1607. English Merchantmen of the size and date of the *Godspeed* 40 tons, *Susan Constant* 100 tons, and the "pinnesse" *Discovery* 20 tons maneuvering for anchorage off Jamestown Island 1607. *A pencil Study by Griffith Bailey Coale, courtesy of Mariners Museum.*

Worship at Cape Henry on April 29, 1607 as depicted by Stephen Reid.
Courtesy of the Chrysler Museum at Norfolk.

Pottery-making as it may have been done in the early years at Jamestown where such work was carried on. *A painting by Sidney King for Colonial National Historical Park.*

"The Cooper" as he may have worked in early Jamestown. A painting by Sidney King for Colonial National Historical Park.

Shipbuilding, known to have been carried on at Jamestown as early as 1609, may have been done in this manner. *A painting by Sidney King for Colonial National Historical Park.*

A winter scene suggestive of life on Jamestown Island about 1625. *From a painting by Sidney King for Colonial National Historical Park.*

A home such as could have existed at Jamestown by 1625. *From a painting for Colonial National Historical Park by Sidney King.*

Virginia, 1607-1624

On May 13, 1607, three small English ships approached Jamestown Island in Virginia: the *Susan Constant* of 100 tons, commanded by Captain Christopher Newport and carrying seventy-one persons; the *Godspeed* of forty tons, commanded by Captain Bartholomew Gosnold and carrying fifty-two persons; and the *Discovery*, a pinnace of twenty tons, under Captain John Ratcliffe with twenty-one persons. During the day they maneuvered the ships so close to the shore that they were "moored to the trees in six fathom [of] water." The next day, May 14, George Percy continues, "we landed all our men, which were set to worke about the fortification, others some to watch and ward as it was convenient." In this manner the first permanent English settlement in America was begun on the shores of the James River, in Virginia, about twenty years after the ill-fated attempts to establish a colony on Roanoke Island and thirteen years before the Pilgrims made their historic landing at Plymouth in New England.

THE START OF COLONIZATION

The expedition of 1607, dispatched by the Virginia Company of London, included supplies and no less than 145 persons of whom 104 or 105 (depending on which of the more detailed contemporary accounts is accepted) were to remain in Virginia as the first settlers. The fleet left England late in 1606. It moved down the Thames River from London on December 20 and, after a slow start, the ships proceeded over the long route through the West Indies. Captain Newport was in command, and the identity of the councilors who were to govern in Virginia lay hidden in a locked box not to be opened until their destination had been reached.

1

Dissension at one point on the voyage led to charges against John Smith who reached the New World in confinement. This was suggestive of the later personal and group feuds and disagreements that plagued the first years of the Virginia Colony. It was a condition that grew out of the initial organization that placed authority in Virginia in a Council rather than in a single governor. It led John Rolfe, in 1616, to write, in retrospect, that: "the beginning of this plantacion was governed by a President & Councell aristocraticallie. The President yerely chosen out of the Councell, which consisted of twelve persons. This government lasted above two yeres: in which time such envie, dissentions and jarrs were daily sowen amongst them, that they choaked the seedes and blasted the fruits of all mens labors."

The "Land of Virginia" was first seen by the lookout on April 26, and just a little later in the same day a party was sent ashore at Cape Henry to make what was the first landing in the wilderness which they came to conquer. Having been aboard ship for many weeks, the settlers found the expanse of land, the green virgin trees, the cool, fresh water, and the unspoiled landscape a pleasant view to behold. At Cape Henry they saw Indians and several of the party were wounded by their arrows, notably Capt. Gabriel Archer, one of the experienced leaders.

They built a "shallop," went exploring into the country for short distances by land and water, enjoyed the spring flowers, and tasted roasted oysters and "fine beautiful strawberries." On April 29, a cross was set up among the sand dunes. The next day the ships were moved from Cape Henry into Chesapeake Bay to the site on Hampton Roads which they named Point Comfort, now Old Point Comfort.

For about two weeks, explorations were made along both banks of the James, below and above Jamestown, from its mouth to a point as far upstream perhaps as the mouth of the Appomattox River near present Hopewell. Parties went ashore to investigate promising areas, and communication was established with the native tribes. On May 12, a point of land at the mouth of Archer's Hope, now College Creek, a little below Jamestown, was examined in detail. From this site the ships moved directly to Jamestown, where they arrived May 13. On May 14, they landed and broke ground for the fort and the town that ultimately won the distinction of the first permanent English settlement in America and the Capital of the Virginia Colony for almost a century.

In May 1607, the days were warm; the nights, cool. Life was stirring in the wilderness and nature had been generous, the colonists thought. There were fruits, abundant timber, deer and other animals for food, and a not too numerous native population. The hot, humid weather of midsummer and the snow, ice, and emptiness of winter were not in evidence. The choice of a site for settlement was both good and bad. The anchorage for ships at Jamestown was good. The Island had not then become a true island and had an easily controlled dry land isthmus connection with the mainland. As the river narrows here, it was one of the best control points on the James. It had been abandoned by the Indians; and it was a bit inland, hence somewhat out of range of the Spanish menace. Arable land on the Island was limited by inlets and "guts." The marshes bred in abundance, even the deadly mosquitoes whose forebears had been brought from the West Indies in the colonists' own vessels; and, with contamination so easy, drinking water was a problem. All of these facts became evident to these first English Americans as the months went by.

When the orders were opened after arrival in Virginia, it was found that the governing body in the Colony was made up of seven councilors. Edward Maria Wingfield, of gallant service in the Low Countries; Bartholomew Gosnold and Christopher Newport, both seasoned seamen and captains; John Ratcliffe, who piloted the *Discovery* to Virginia; John Martin, an earlier commander under Drake; John Smith, already an experienced adventurer; and George Kendall, a cousin of Sir Edwin Sandys who later was to play a dominant role in the Virginia Company. To this list

3

can be added other prominent names: George Percy, brother to the Earl of Northumberland and a trained sailor; Gabriel Archer, a lawyer who had already explored in the New England country; and Reverend Robert Hunt, the vicar at Jamestown, whose pious and exemplary living was noted by his associates.

THE ESTABLISHMENT OF JAMESTOWN

The work of establishing Jamestown and of exploring the country round about began almost simultaneously and remarkable strides were made in a short time. The several weeks between May 13 and June 22, when Newport left Virginia for a return to England, were busy ones. At Jamestown an area was cleared of trees and the fort begun. The soil was readied and the English wheat brought over for the purpose was planted. At this point Newport, in one of the small boats, led an exploring party as far as the falls of the James. He was absent from Jamestown about a week and returned to find that the Indians had launched a fierce attack on the new settlement which had been saved, perhaps, by the fact that the ships were near at hand. These afforded safe quarters and carried cannon on their decks that had a frightening effect on the natives.

The fort was completed about mid-June. It was triangular in shape, with a "bulwarke" at each corner which was shaped like a "halfe moone." Within the "bulwarkes" were mounted four or five pieces of artillery: demiculverins which fired balls of about nine pounds in weight. The fort enclosed about one acre with its river side extending 420 feet and its other sides measuring 300 feet. The principal gate faced the river and was in the south side (curtain) of the fort, although there were other openings, one at each "bulwarke," and each was protected by a piece of ordnance. The church, storehouse, and living quarters were flimsily built of perishable materials, within the walls of the palisaded fort, along fixed "streets" and around an open yard. For the first few years this fort was Jamestown.

Before the fort was completed the wheat had come up and was growing nicely, as George Percy wrote in what was probably the first essay on farming along the James River. About June 10, John Smith, partly through the intercession of Robert Hunt, was released and admitted to his seat on the Council. Relations with the Indians improved. On June 21, the third Sunday after Trinity, the first recorded Anglican communion was celebrated. "We had comunion. Captain Newport dined ashore with our diet, and invited many of us to supper as a farewell." The next day, Christopher Newport raised anchor and began the return trip to England. He took letters from those remaining in Virginia and carried accounts describing Virginia and the events that had occurred. The settlement had been made, and the future seemed promising.

SUMMER AND FALL, 1607

Within the short span of two months, conditions changed drastically. The Indians became cautious and distrustful, and provisions, not sufficiently augmented from the country, began to run low. Spoilage destroyed some food, and, with the coming of the hot, humid weather, the brackish drinking water proved dangerous. In August, death struck often and quickly, taking among others the stabilizing hand of Captain Gosnold. Inexperience, unwillingness, or inability due to insufficient food, to do the hard work that was necessary and the lack of sufficient information about how to survive in a primeval wilderness led to bickering, disagreements, and, to what was more serious still, inaction.

As the first summer wore on it was natural that hostility should develop toward the titular head of the Colony. Had the first president, Edward Maria Wingfield, been a stronger, more adventurous, and more daring man, conditions might have been a little better, despite his lack of real authority. He was not the leader to act, and, to reason later. Consequently, opinion was arrayed against him and charges, some unjust no doubt, were formed that

5

led to his deposition and replacement in one of the two celebrated jury trials which occurred at Jamestown about mid-September. His successor, perhaps no more able, was John Ratcliffe who continued for about a year until he was deposed and replaced by Matthew Scrivener, one of those who came over with the first supply. It was a little later, in 1608, that Captain John Smith took the helm as chief councilor, which was what the president really was. It was under the presidency of Ratcliffe, however, that Smith emerged as an able, experienced leader, who preferred action to inaction even though it might be questioned later. His work and his decisions, sometimes wise, sometimes not so wise, did much to insure the initial survival of the Colony.

When the first cool days of approaching autumn touched Jamestown, in 1607, spirits rose and hopefulness supplanted despair. Disease, which had reduced the number to less than fifty persons, subsided; the oppressive heat lessened; and Indian crops of peas, corn, and beans began to mature. Friendly relations were established with the natives, and barter trade developed. As the leaves fell, game became easier to get, ducks multiplied in the ponds and marshes, and life in general seemed brighter. Work was resumed in preparation for the coming winter, and exploration was undertaken.

It was in December, 1607, while investigating the Chickahominy River area, that Smith was taken by the Indians. He was eventually carried before Powhatan who released him, some say through the intercession of the young Pocahontas. Upon return to Jamestown he was caught in the meshes of a feuding Council and was faced even with the possibility of being hanged for the death of his companions.

The Three Supplies, 1608-1610

All was forgotten early in January, however, when Newport reached Jamestown with the first supply for the settlers. He brought food, equipment, instructions, and news from home. The two ships of the supply had left England together, but the second did not reach Virginia until April.

Shortly after Newport's arrival in January, disaster came. Fire swept through "James Fort," consuming habitations, provisions, ammunition, some of the palisades and even Reverend Robert Hunt's books. This was a serious blow in the face of winter weather. With the help of Newport and his sailors, the church, storehouse, palisades, and cabins were partially rebuilt before he sailed again for England early in April. Much more could have been done had he not consumed so many days in a pompous visit and lengthy negotiations with the wily Powhatan. Then, too, the ships had to be loaded for the return voyage, for the London backers were calling loudly for profitable produce.

The first of the spring months were spent in cutting cedar logs and preparing "clapboards" for sale in England, and a little later there seems to have been a mild "gold rush" at Jamestown as some hopeful looking golden colored soil was found. This all delayed early spring clearing and planting, and boded ill for the coming summer when Smith undertook additional explorations.

It was in September 1608 that Smith became president in fact and inaugurated a program of physical improvement at Jamestown. The area about the fort was enlarged and the standing structures repaired. At this point, in October, the second supply arrived, including seventy settlers, who, when added to the survivors in Virginia, raised the over-all population to about 120.

Among the new arrivals were two women, Mistress Forrest and her maid. Several months later, in the church at Jamestown, the maid, Ann Burras, was married to one of the settlers, John Laydon, a carpenter by trade. This marriage has been ranked as "the first recorded English marriage on the soil of the United States." Their child, Virginia, born the next year, was the first to be born at Jamestown.

With the second supply came workmen sent over to produce

glass, pitch, soap ashes, and other items profitable in England. So rapidly did they begin the search for a source of wealth that "trials" of at least some of the products were sent home when Newport left Jamestown before the end of the year.

In addition to settlers and supplies, Newport brought more instructions from the Company officials. The Colony was not succeeding financially, and it was urged that the Council spend more time in planning the preparation of marketable products. It was urged, too, that gold be sought more actively; that Powhatan be crowned as a recognition befitting his position; and that more effort be expended in search of the Roanoke settlers. These projects, all untimely, were emphasized, and the more pressing needs of adequate shelter and sufficient food were neglected.

In the interval from about February to May 1609, there was considerable material progress in and about Jamestown. Perhaps forty acres were cleared and prepared for planting in Indian corn, the new grain that fast became a staple commodity. A "deep well" was dug in the fort. The church was re-covered and twenty cabins built. A second trial was made at glass manufacture in the furnaces built late in 1608. A blockhouse was built at the isthmus which connected the Island to the mainland for better control of the Indians, and a new fort was erected on a tidal creek across the river from Jamestown.

Smith was now in command, as his fellow councilors either had returned to England or were dead. About this time there came a new disaster. With all attention centered on the numerous construction projects, insufficient protection was given the meager supply of grain. When discovered, rats had consumed almost all of the vital corn stores. Faced with this situation, Smith found it necessary to scatter the settlers, sending some to live with the Indians and some to eat at the oyster banks. Only "a small guarde of gentlemen & some others [were left] about the president at James Towne."

In midsummer of 1609, conditions at Jamestown were not good, although it is doubtful that they were any worse than during the two previous summers. The settlers were becoming acclimated, and they were learning the ways of the new country. Supplies were low, yet the number of colonists was small, and a good harvest and a good fall might have improved matters had not some 400 new, inexperienced settlers sailed into the James with only damaged supplies. To add to other complications, they brought fever and plague. In the selection of prospective settlers for the voyage the standards had been low, and too many ne'er-do-wells, and even renegades, had been included.

This was the third supply, and it reached Jamestown in August. Unfortunately it arrived without its leadership and the authority to institute the governmental changes which the Company had authorized. These changes provided for the appointment by the Company of a strong governor with an advisory council in Virginia. Sir Thomas Gates had been dispatched as Governor, yet the ship bearing him, along with Sir George Somers and Captain Newport was wrecked in the Bermuda Islands.

Reaching Virginia in the third supply were several men who had been earlier leaders in the Colony and who were now all hostile to Smith: Archer, Ratcliffe, and Martin. A confusing scene developed over command. The old leaders, particularly Smith, refused to give way to the new in the absence of Gates, the appointed governor. There was considerable bickering which led to an uneasy settlement, leaving Smith in charge for the duration of his yearly term, now almost expired.

It was obvious to everyone that there were too many men for all to remain at Jamestown. John Martin was sent to attempt a settlement at Nansemond, on the south side of the James below Jamestown, while Captain Francis West, brother of Lord De La Warr, was sent to settle at the falls of the James. Returning to Jamestown after an inspection tour at the falls, Captain Smith was injured by burning gunpowder and incapacitated. Ratcliffe, Archer, and Martin seemingly used this opportunity to depose him and to compel him to return to England to face their charges against him as had been the fate of previous presidents. These three men, failing to agree on a replacement from their own number, persuaded George Percy to accept the position of president. Percy was in command during the terrible winter that followed.

The winter of 1609-10 has been described through the years as the "starving time," seemingly, an accurate description. It saw the population shrink from 500 to about sixty as a result of disease, sickness, Indian arrows, and malnutrition. It destroyed morale and reduced the men to scavengers stalking the forest, fields, and woods for anything that might be used as food. When spring came there was little spirit left in the settlement. It would seem unjust to attribute the disaster to Percy, who did what he could to ameliorate conditions by attempting trade and keeping the men busy. The "starving time" appears to have been caused by an accumulation of circumstances not the least of them being internal dissension and the now open hostility of the Indian. The heavy use of force and armed persuasion in dealing with them was bound to have its effect. It cut off the badly needed supply of corn and other Indian foods.

A Critical Hour

In May 1610, the hearts of the weary settlers were gladdened when Sir Thomas Gates, their new governor, sailed into the James. For about a year he and the survivors of the wreck of the *Sea Venture* had labored in Bermuda to make possible the continuation of their voyage to Virginia. For the purpose they built two small boats, the *Patience* and the *Deliverance*. It was not a pleasant sight that greeted them at Jamestown. Ruin and desolation were everywhere. Gates, with his Council, on July 7, 1610, wrote that Jamestown seemed "raither as the ruins of some auntient [for]tification, then that any people living might now inhabit it. . . ."

Gates promptly distributed provisions, such as he had, and introduced a code of martial law, the code that was strengthened later by De La Warr and made famous by its strict enforcement during the governorship of Sir Thomas Dale. After surveying the condition of the settlement and realizing that the supplies he had brought would not last three weeks, Gates took counsel with the leaders. They decided to abandon the settlement. On June 7, 1610, the settlers, except some of the Poles and Dutchmen who were with Powhatan, boarded the ship, left Jamestown, and started down the James.

The next morning, while still in the river, advance word reached Gates that Lord De La Warr had arrived at Point Comfort on the way to Jamestown and was bringing 150 settlers and a generous supply. The bad news carried to England by the returning ships of the third supply, late in 1609, had caused considerable stir in Virginia Company circles and had resulted in De La Warr's decision to go to Virginia. Learning of the new supply, Gates hastened back to Jamestown. The new settlement had been saved in a manner that was recognized at that time as an act of "Providence."

On June 10, De La Warr reached "James Citty" and made his landing. He entered the fort through the south gate, and, with his colors flying, went on to the church where Reverend Richard Buck delivered an impressive sermon. Then his ensign, Anthony Scott, read his commission, and Gates formally delivered to him his own authority as governor. De La Warr's arrival had given the settlement new life and new hope. Lean times lay ahead, yet the most difficult years lay behind. Virginia now had a government that made for stability under the governor, and the old settlers, who, a little later, came to be called "ancient planters," had learned well by experience.

11

Gates, after dealing with the Indians, left for England. De La Warr, who continued to live aboard ship for a time, called a Council, reorganized the colonists, and directed operations to promote the welfare of the Colony, including the construction of two forts near Point Comfort. He fell sick, however, and, after a long illness, was forced to leave Jamestown and Virginia in March 1611. The now veteran administrator, George Percy, was made governor in charge. With De La Warr went Dr. Lawrence Bohun, who had experimented extensively with the curative powers of plants and herbs at Jamestown.

Order and More Stable Ways

In May, 1611 Sir Thomas Dale, on military leave from his post in the Low Countries, arrived as deputy governor of Virginia. With him were three ships, three smaller boats, 300 people, domestic animals, and supplies. He proceeded to give form and substance to the martial law which had been evoked by his predecessors and to the achievement of rather severe regimentation. He began by posting proclamations "for the publique view" at Jamestown. Later, he thoroughly inspected suitable settlement sites and surveyed conditions generally. He wrote, on May 25, that on arrival at Jamestown he found ". . . no corn sett, some few seeds put into a private garden or two; but the cattle, cows, goats, swine, poultry &c to be well and carefully on all hands preserved and all in good plight and likeing."

To get things in order at the seat of government, one party was designated to repair the church, another to work on the stable, another to build a wharf. When things were reasonably well in hand at Jamestown, he made plans to push the decision to open a new settlement above Jamestown which, he hoped, would become the real center of the Colony. The reasons for such a removal of the seat of government are well known: not sufficient high land at Jamestown, poor drinking water, too much marsh, and a location not far enough upstream to be out of reach of the Spanish. Too often the reality of the ever present Spanish threat to Virginia is overlooked. Spain, still strong, had long been dominant in the New World and had known intentions of eliminating the English. That they never effectively moved in this direction did not lessen the fear in the Colony in the early years. This explains the various alarms that went out along the James from time to time. Quite naturally there was concern when spies were landed at Point Comfort in 1611. These were kept under careful scrutiny for several years, until disposition was made of them.

In the very critical period of 1611-1616, during the administrations of Gates and Dale, emphasis was away from Jamestown. Emphasis fell on newly established Henrico and then on Bermuda together with their related settlements. Attention was given, too, to Kecoughtan and a settlement was made even on the Eastern Shore. Despite all of this, Jamestown remained as Virginia's capital. In 1612, "Master George Percie . . . [was busy] with the keeping of Jamestown" while much of the Colony had been "moved up river." The first settlement now was looked upon as chiefly a place of safety for hogs and cattle.

In 1614 it was made up of "two faire rowes of howses, all of framed timber, two stories, and an upper garret or corne loft high, besides three large, and substantiall storehowses joined togeather in length some hundred and twenty foot, and in breadth forty. . . ." Without the town ". . . in the Island [were] some very pleasant, and beutifull howses, two blockhowses . . . and certain other framed howses." In 1616 it was a post of fifty under the command of Lieutenant John Sharpe, who was acting in the absence of Captain Francis West. Thirty-one of these were "farmors" and all maintained themselves with "food and raiment."

The Gates-Dale five-year administration (1611-16) actually saw Virginia established as a going concern. The role of Dale in all of this seems to have been a heavy, perhaps the predominant, one although the role of Gates should not be overlooked. Martial law brought order and uniformity in operations and compelled the people to work regularly, the hours being six to ten in the morning, two to four in the afternoon. Dale saw to it that corn was planted and harvested, that houses and boats were built, and that the new laws were strictly observed. He pressed one and all into service, even the women, some of whom "were appointed to make shirtes for the Colony servants" using carefully rationed needle and thread. Dale was credited, by a contemporary, as building on the foundations laid by Gates in a manner that dealt effectively with the two greatest "enemies and disturbers of our proceedings": "enmity with the naturalls, and . . . famine." Among the important achievements was the careful husbanding of livestock to the end that a "great stock of kine, goates, and other cattle" was built up for the company "for the service of the publique."

Both Gates and Dale proceeded with a stern attitude toward the Indians. In the end it was possible to arrive at a peaceful state by force and negotiation. Dale recognized, too, that the Pocahontas-John Rolfe marriage, in 1614, was "an other knot to binde this peace the stronger." This helped to strengthen the treaties worked out with old Powhatan and with the closer Chickahominies.

So effective were all of these measures that John Rolfe, in 1616, wrote "whereupon a peace was concluded, which still continues so firme, that our people yearly plant and reape quietly, and travell in the woods a fowling and a hunting as freely and securely from danger or treacherie as in England. The great blessings of God have followed this peace, and it, next under him, hath bredd our plentie. . . ."

All this was accomplished when the fortunes of the Virginia Company were at a low point and little support was being sent to the Colony. John Rolfe then went on to predict that Dale's "worth and name . . . will out last the standing of this planta-tion. . . ."

Martial law, strictly administered at first, was gradually re-laxed in application as conditions stabilized. Prior to 1614 Dale took the momentous step of allotting "to every man in the Col-ony [excepting the Bermuda Hundred people], three English acres of cleere corne ground, which every man is to manure and tend, being in the nature of farmers." Along with the three acres went exemption from much Company service and such as was required was not to be in "seede time, or in harvest." There was, however, to be a yearly levy of "two barrels and a halfe of corne" and, except for clothing, a loss of right to draw on the Company store. This greatly advanced individual responsibility and was a big step toward the evolution of private property. In the be-ginning all ownership was Company controlled. The reason for this is evident. The colonists could not provide food and other necessaries all at once in a wilderness infested by savages. A store-house, or as it was termed, "a magazine," was provided in which all supplies were placed, and to which all products obtained from the land were brought. This was a safety measure, both for the Company, which had expended much for supplies, and for the settlers. This plan has been misunderstood frequently by writers. It did have its disadvantages. In time, with growth, and increased production, the system passed away. The general division of land, promised in 1609, was not to come until 1619. Dale took an interim step that had far reaching importance in establishing permanency and stability.

Gates and Dale in their administration had the help of other enterprising and daring early Virginians such as Samuel Argall, John Rolfe, the Reverend Alexander Whitaker, Ralph Hamor and others. In the case of Captain Samuel Argall, criticism of his later work as governor often beclouds his earlier helpfulness in getting Virginia established. He pioneered in making a direct crossing of the Atlantic to save time and to avoid the Spanish.

Argall led in exploration, both in Virginia waters and northward along the coastline. He was adept at shipbuilding and in the Indian trade. It was evidently he who discovered the best fishing seasons and the fact that the fish made "runs" in the bay and in the rivers. He made open attack on the French settlements to the north in New England and Nova Scotia, returning to Jamestown with his captives. There is little wonder that a contemporary wrote, "Captain Argal whose indevores in this action intitled him most worthy."

It was Argall, too, who, while on a trading expedition on the Potomac, captured Pocahontas and brought her prisoner to Jamestown in an attempt to deal with her father, Powhatan. She was well received at Jamestown, where earlier she had often visited, and when her father refused to pay the price asked for her ransom, she was detained. Later, she preferred life with the English and did not wish to return to her native village. She was placed under the tutelage of Reverend Alexander Whitaker who instructed her in the Christian faith. Eventually she was baptized, and, in April 1614, in the church at Jamestown, married John Rolfe.

This was a reflection of the religious concern that existed in Virginia. One of the ministers, Alexander Whitaker reported: That: "Sir Thomas Dale (with whom I am) is a man of great knowledge in divinity, and of a good conscience in all his doings: both which bee rare in a martiall man. Every Sabbath day wee preach in the forenoone, and chatechize in the afternoone. Every Saturday at night I exercise in Sir Thomas Dales house. Our Church affaires bee consulted on by the minister, and foure of the most religious men. Once every moneth wee have a communion, and once a yeer a solemn fast."

TOBACCO

It was John Rolfe who pioneered in the cultivation of the plant that was to be Virginia's economic salvation, tobacco. In

16

the first years of the settlement every effort had been made to find products in the New World that would assure financial success for the settlers and the Company. Pitch, tar, timber, sassafras, cedar, and other natural products were sent in the returning ships. Attempts to produce glass on a paying scale proved futile, as did early efforts to make silk, using the native mulberry trees growing in abundance. The glass furnaces fell into disuse, and rats ate the silkworms. Even the native tobacco plant (*Nicotiana rustica*), found growing wild, was, as William Strachey reported, ". . . not of the best kind . . . [but was] poore and weake, and of a biting tast . . ." and initially held little promise.

It was about 1610-11 that seed was imported into Virginia from the island of Trinidad very probably at the hand of John Rolfe, an ardent smoker, who was credited by Ralph Hamor as the pioneer English colonist in regularly growing tobacco for export. Hence he can be called the father of the American tobacco industry. In its initial stage, too, there was encouragement from the experienced Captain George Yeardley.

Following the process of selection and crossing which had proved so successful for the Spanish cultivators in the West Indies, the initial efforts were rewarding. The new plant (*Nicotiana tabacum*) proved easily naturalized and adaptable to the Virginia soil.

The initial success led to an experimental shipment of tobacco from Virginia in 1613. This was of pleasing taste and was well received in some quarters. Soon tract after tract was cleaned of its native *Nicotiana rustica* as the settlers turned to the promising new species. For a few years production was slow since English dealers were reluctant to hazard too much on an uncertain commodity. In the 1615-16 period Spain sent tobacco into London at the rate of twenty-five pounds for each of the 2,300 pounds coming from Virginia. This was not to continue, however, since English leaders were growing hostile to the successful Spanish trade. Even before becoming aware of the Virginia product, they

17

were, with some success, encouraging production in England itself.

Despite domestic tobacco, however, and the favor of Spanish leaf, the Virginia product, cheaper than the Spanish, began to win friendly users in London and in the other cities. To meet the demand and to produce profits, the young colony all but abandoned other industries and even its staples, to the concern of the Company, for the cultivation of "the weed." Soon governors were taking measures to restrict planting in the interest of producing foodstuffs and in defending themselves. Captain Samuel Argall, who came to Jamestown in 1617, is said to have found "but five or six houses, the church downe, the palizado's broken, the bridge in pieces, the well of fresh water spoiled; the store-house . . . used for the church; the marketplace, and streets, and all other spare places planted with tobacco; the salvages as frequent in their homes as themselves, whereby they were become expert in our armes . . . the Colonie dispersed all about planting Tobacco." In 1617 Virginia exported some 20,000 pounds, in 1619 this had doubled and in 1629, only a decade and a half after the first shipment, the total reached 1,500,000 pounds.

Thus, a new trade and industry were born in the Colony. Tobacco proved to be the economic salvation of Virginia, and provided a means that brought land into use and made slavery profitable. Tobacco and slavery together led to the development of important characteristics of the whole social, political, and economic structure of the Old South. One of the immediate effects of tobacco culture in Virginia was the impetus it gave to the expansion of the area of settlement and to the number of settlers coming to Virginia.

YEARDLEY AND ARGALL

When Dale departed Virginia in May, 1616 there was more security, stability, good management, deeper understanding of the new land, and a keener knowledge of survival than had existed prior to this date. Even so, at this time only about 350 of all the hundreds of persons who had come to the Colony had managed to stay alive and remained here.

Captain George Yeardley was left in charge, seemingly having been appointed directly by Dale. Under him, it was reported, "the Colony lived in peace and best plentie that ever it was to that time." He very probably was glad to see the supply ship that came in October, 1616. Various kinds of provisions from it were exchanged with the colonists for their tobacco. It was this ship, too, that brought Abraham Piercey who, as "cape-merchant," took over the management of the Company's store in Virginia.

But all was not peace. Yeardley had soon to deal with the Chickahominies who objected to their payment of "tribute corn." This was soon resolved to the satisfaction of the Governor. Later there was friendly exchange with the Indians even, it seems, to the extent of training some in the use of firearms for hunting purposes and "There were divers . . . [that] had savages in like manner for their men." Perhaps, there was too much familiarity for later well being.

In May, 1618 Argall returned to Virginia as deputy governor in charge. He seemingly, with "sense and industry," began to renovate the disrepair he found, particularly at Jamestown. He was the first to prescribe the limits of Jamestown as well as of "the *corporation* and *parish*" of which it was the chief seat. He soon re-established good relations with Opechancanough now the dominant Indian personality. He was hampered by a great drought and a severe storm that damaged corn and tobacco, and he sought to control profit and tobacco prices by proclamation. Moreover, he was the author of a policy of watchfulness and carefulness in individual relationships with the Indians.

Eventually, however, Argall was severely criticized and accused of the misappropriation of Company resources. He was charged, too, with a host of private wrongs to particular persons, wrongs accompanied by high-handed actions. Much in disfavor, he slipped away from the Colony a matter of days before the new Governor, Sir George Yeardley again, reached Virginia in April, 1619.

It was early in the Yeardley-Argall three year span (1616-19) that a new form of settlement began to take root in Virginia. This was that of the particular plantation. No new Company communities had been, or would be, added to the "four ancient boroughs" ("Incorporations") already established, yet many would rise as the result of the enterprise, expenditure, and direction of special ("particular") persons, or groups, within the Company or having the sanction of it. Such settlements were known as particular plantations.

Resulting settlements spread east and west along the James and outward along its rivers and creeks as well. Jamestown lay approximately in the center of an expanding and growing Colony. It was the center of one of the four initial Incorporations and it was more. It developed into one of the original Virginia shires in 1634. This shire, a decade later, became a county. James City County continues as the oldest governing unit in English America. Jamestown was its chief seat, Virginia's capital town and the principal center of the Colony's social and political life. In size it remained small, yet it was intimately and directly related to all of the significant developments of Virginia in the period.

There is strong evidence that Jamestown was the first to feel the impact of the advantages and fruits that growth produced. Material progress is evident as early as 1619 in the letter of John Pory, Secretary of the Colony, written from Virginia late in that year:

Nowe that your lordship may knowe, that we are not the veriest beggars in the worlde, our cowekeeper here of James citty on Sunday goes accowtered all in freshe flaming silke; and a wife of one that in England had professed the black arte, not of a schollar, but of a collier of Croydon, weares her rought bever hatt with a faire perle hatband, and a silken suite thereto correspondent.

But it is good to remember, perhaps, that Virginia was still not the perfect paradise. On March 15, 1619 a letter reaching England reported sad news and very likely not unusual news—"about 300 of the Inhabitants . . . died this last yeare."

A NEW APPROACH

In 1618 there were internal changes and dissensions in the Virginia Company that led to the resignation of Sir Thomas Smith, as Treasurer, and to the election of Sir Edwin Sandys as his successor. This roughly corresponded to changes in Company policy toward the administration of the Colony and to intensified efforts to develop Virginia. It led to the abolition of martial law, to the establishment of property ownership, to greater individual freedom and participation in matters of government and to the intensification of economic effort. The program was prompted by a desire to make the Virginia enterprise a financial success, to increase the population, and to make the Colony attractive as well as to give the colonists more of a sense of participation.

Sir George Yeardley, recently knighted, returned to Virginia as Governor, in April 1619, and was the first spokesman in the Colony for the new policy toward Virginia. In England it had been ably advanced on behalf of the Colony by Sir Edwin Sandys, the Earl of Southampton, and John and Nicholas Ferrar.

Land was one of the great sources of wealth in Virginia and soon after early commercial enterprise failed, was recognized as such. Its acquisition became a prime objective. Initially the Company had determined that no land would be assigned to planters, or adventurers, until the expiration of a seven year period. And this period was in actual practice delayed. The first real, or general, "division" was provided for in 1618 and this became effective in Virginia in 1619.

It was recognized that there were several groups meriting land.

First came the Company and its investors. The second was the particular hundreds and plantations sponsored and belonging to private adventurers joined in investing groups in England. The third was composed of individual planters who lived and resided in Virginia. Yeardley came armed with instructions to effect the division. The boundaries of the four Incorporations (James City, Charles City, Henrico and Kecoughtan) were to be fixed and public lands for the support of their officers and churches were to be set aside as well as tracts for Company officials in Virginia and others for Company use and profit. The consolidation of all settlements into the four listed "Cities or Burroughs" was soon consummated.

Two classifications of planters were noted—those who came to Virginia before Dale departed in 1616 and those who came later. The first group, called "ancient planters," may have been Virginia's first "aristocracy." Each such person with three years of residence was entitled to 100 acres as a "first division." Those having come to Virginia after Dale's departure were in a different position. If they had come, or were to come, at their own charge they were to obtain only fifty acres at the "first division." If transported by the Company they were first to serve as "tenants" on the Company's land for a term of seven years.

All grants it was specified would "be made with equal favour except the difference of rent." Rent proved to be a diverse term covering tobacco, capons, merchantable Indian corn and such. Rent payments were a matter of concern and led the planters in the Assembly of 1619 to petition for the appointment of an officer in Virginia to receive them. Payment to the Company in London, in money, was described as impossible.

All tracts, including those allotted prior to the general division, now would have to be laid off and surveyed. The prescribing of bounds became a necessity to resolve existing, and to prevent future, uncertainties and disputes. This was to be the function of William Claiborne, surveyor-general, who reached Virginia in October, 1621.

Headrights were another matter which entered the picture in these formative years. This began as a device, a good one it proved to be, used by the Company to stimulate immigration and settlement in Virginia. It allowed any person who paid his own way to the Colony to receive fifty acres for his own "personal adventure." In addition he could collect fifty acres for each person whose passage he paid. If a person brought himself and three others, for example, he could claim 200 acres under this arrangement. This headright system was later adopted in other colonies and continued in use for generations.

The early success of the land division can be seen, perhaps in the report of John Rolfe written in January, 1620:

All the ancient planters being sett free have chosen places for their dividendes according to the commission, Which giveth all greate content, for now knowing their owne landes, they strive and are prepared to build houses & to cleere their groundes ready to plant, which giveth . . . [them] greate incouragement, and the greatest hope to make the Colony florrish that ever yet happened to them.

Participation in the affairs of government was another element in the new Company approach. Soon after his arrival, Yeardley issued a call for the first representative legislative assembly in America which convened at Jamestown on July 30, 1619, and remained in session until August 4. This was the beginning of our present system of representative government. The full intent behind the moves that led to this historic meeting may never be known. It seems to have been another manifestation of the determination to give those Englishmen in America the rights and privileges of Englishmen at home that had been guaranteed to them in the original Company charter. It seems to be this rather than a planned attempt to establish self-goverment in the New World on a scale that might have been in violation of English law and custom at the time. Whatever the motive, the significance of this meeting in the church at Jamestown remains the same. This body of duly chosen representatives of the people has continued in existence and its evolution leads directly to our State legislatures and to the Congress of the United States.

Circumstances seemed to prevent the annual meeting of the Assembly even though this was initially intended. Possibly, although it is not clear, the Assembly met in March, 1620. There was a session after the arrival of Governor Wyatt in October, 1621 although little is known of its actions. The next session of record was in the late winter of 1624 and of this some papers have survived. At the time the dissolution of the Company seemed to be sensed and the Burgesses acted carefully. Much of the session was devoted to answering questions relative to the state of the Colony. The Assembly went on record, too, denouncing the so-called autocratic government that existed in Virginia prior to 1619. There was, however, refusal to associate its name with an attack on the Company and it would not send its papers to England by the investigating commissioners. Instead they were sent by a representative of the Assembly's choice. The status of the General Assembly under the King, when Virginia became a royal colony, was, for sometime, undefined and even its continuation was, perhaps, doubtful. It did, nonetheless, survive to become a chief instrument of government.

In the social field the Company had recognized that homes, children and family life make for stability and now steps were taken to do something about it. To this end, in November 1619, a program was launched to increase the emigration of women to Virginia. Many had already come to contribute greatly to the Colony's welfare, the first two in 1608; and family life was already very much a reality. The male percentage of the population was, however, still much too high.

The first of the "maids" sent in this new program reached Virginia in late May and early June, 1620 seemingly to the benfit of both "maids" and eligible bachelors. In 1621 it was reported

24

that in December the *Warwick* arrived with "an extraordinary choice lot [of] thirty-eight maids for wives."

Earlier, in August 1619, there had been another event, this an unplanned one, when a group of negroes were brought to the Colony out of the West Indies and sold from the ship which brought them for "victualls." This created little attention at the time. Evidently these newcomers found themselves bound for a time as servants rather than as slaves. The matter of mass negro slavery with its profitableness in the tobacco economy was, as yet, decades away. This event of 1619, however, may properly be noted as the first move in this direction.

Immigration to the Colony continued to increase including even a number of English youths, and measures were taken to meet the religious and educational needs of the settlers. This was the period that saw the attempt to establish a college at Henrico.

The reorganized Virginia Company, following its political changes, renewed its efforts to expand the Colony and to stimulate profitable employment. Heavy emphasis was placed on crop diversification and on the establishment of a number of new industries including forest products, wine, iron and glass, the latter attempted a second time possibly on Glasshouse Point just outside of Jamestown Island. The planting of mulberry trees and the growing of silkworms were advanced by the dispatch of treatises on silk culture as well as silkworm eggs in a project in which King James I himself had a personal interest.

The industrial and manufacturing efforts of these years, however, were not destined to succeed. This condition was not due to any laxity on the part of George Sandys, resident Treasurer in Virginia, who was something of an economic on-the-spot supervisor for the Company. Virginia could not yet support these projects profitably, and interest was lacking on the part of the planters who found in tobacco a source of wealth superior to anything else that had been tried. It was the profit from tobacco that supported the improved living conditions that came throughout the Colony.

These Englishmen who came to settle in the wilderness retained their desire for the advantages of life in England. Books, for example, were highly valued, and with the passage of the years were no uncommon commodity in Virginia. As early as 1608, Rev. Robert Hunt had a library at Jamestown, which was consumed by fire in January of that year. Each new group of colonists seemingly added to the store on hand: *Bibles, Books of Common Prayer,* other religious works, medical and scientific treatises, legal publications, accounts of gardening, and such. There was local literary effort, too, such as that by Treasurer George Sandys who continued his celebrated translation of Ovid's *Metamorphoses* in the house of William Pierce at Jamestown.

YEARDLEY AND WYATT

Yeardley, having instituted the measures of the "Greate Charter," continued to serve as Governor until November 18, 1621. His was a good administration, yet it was not without criticism. There was some unfavorable comment on his negotiations relative to Indian lands as well as in the arrangement of various government fees. With so many personal and private interests in so many of the individual settlements, it is remarkable that he did not get into difficulties of a more serious nature. Even when Sir Francis Wyatt relieved him as governor, he continued on as a Councilor and was later to be Governor again. He had been at the helm when Virginia enjoyed, perhaps, its best three years to date—1619-21.

His successor, Wyatt, proved as popular and even survived the dissolution of the Company. Wyatt, as others before and others to follow, found the governorship to be expensive. It is reported that he spent £1,000 in less than two years. Both Yeardley and Wyatt resided at Jamestown from which, for the most part, they directed Colony affairs. Here they maintained a most impressive establishment with their wives, children and indentured servants including some of the negroes now resident in the Colony.

It is in the 1619 to 1624 period that the first clear picture of at least a part of the physical town of Jamestown emerges, for this period corresponds with the earliest known property records that exist. The town had outgrown the original fort in some years past and now appeared as a fairly flourishing settlement. The records reveal that many of the property owners were yeomen, merchants, carpenters, hog-raisers, farmers, joiners, shopkeepers, and ordinary "fellows," as well as colonial officials. The "New Town" section of James City developed in this period as the old section proved too small and the residents began to build more substantial houses, principally frame on brick foundations. Even so, the town was far from that of a city, perhaps, only a village at best. It was, nonetheless, as close to a hub of political, social, and economic life as completely rural Virginia had. It was the Colony's capital in every sense.

The population figures taken in these years give a good idea of the size of Jamestown in this period. In February 1624, it is recorded that 183 persons were living in Jamestown and 35 others on the Island outside of the town proper. These are listed by name, as are the 87 who had died between April 1623 and the following February. In the "census" of January 1625 there was a total of 124 residents listed for "James Citty" and an additional 51 for the Island. The over-all total of 175 included some 122 males and 53 females.

Aside from the population statistics, the musters of January 1625 give much more information. Jamestown had a church, a court-of-guard (guardhouse), 3 stores (probably storehouses), a merchant's store, and 33 houses. Ten of the Colony's 40 boats were here, including a skiff, a "shallop" of 4 tons, and a "barque" of 40 tons. There were stores of fish, 24,880 pounds to be exact, corn, peas, and meal. There were four pieces of ordnance, supplies of powder, shot and lead, and, for individual use, "fixt peeces," snaphances, pistols, seventy swords, coats of mail, quilted coats, and thirty-five suits of armor. The bulk of the Colony's livestock seems to have been localized in the James-town area, about half (183) of the cattle, a little more than half (265) of the hogs, and well over half (126) of the goats. The one horse listed for the Colony was shown to have been at James-town, but in this category the "census" must have been deficient. Even in 1616 there had been 3 horses and 3 mares.

The massacre and its aftermath and the investigation and dis-solution of the Company dominated the Virginia scene in Wyatt's first three year term as Governor. These things should not, per-haps, becloud the continued expansion and growth of the Colony that resumed after the fateful year of 1622 when the massacre was followed, in the summer, with disease along the James and then by the more specific plague.

It was on March 22, 1622 that the great catastrophe struck Virginia in the form of the well planned and carefully executed massacre by the Indians under the crafty leadership of Opechan-canough, successor to Powhatan. Although the consequences were not enough to threaten the survival of the Colony, they were deeply serious. At least a fourth, if not a third, of all resi-dents lay dead at the end of a single day. Many plantations were abandoned and safety and security became the principal order of the day. It spelled the end of numerous projects such as the production of iron and of enterprises such as the attempt to found a college. Jamestown, given timely warning because of the loyalty of an Indian, Chanco, to his master, saw no damage. In this respect it was one of only a few such areas. It did, however, see some resulting congestion as survivors came in from distant, and even nearby, communities.

Regrouping, reorganization and revenge followed after the initial shock was over. Punishment of the Indians occupied the center of the stage for months. In January, 1623, however, the

Governor and his Council could report in answer to Company inquiries, some of which were critical of Colony operations, that "We have anticipated your desires by settinge uppon the Indians in all places." Directed by the Governor from Jamestown, George Sandys, Sir George Yeardley, Capt. John West, Capt. William Powell and others led expeditions against the various native tribes. "In all which places we have slaine divers, burnte theire townes, destroyde theire wears [weirs] & corne." The seizure of considerable additional mature corn, likewise, was a blow to the Indian and a help to the English. The Indian had been brought to heel, yet he was still not impotent, a fact that the colonists now well recognized and of which they had occasional reminder as when Capt. Henry Spelman and his party were slain in April, 1623.

VIRGINIA AND THE DISSOLUTION

The Virginia Company established the first permanent English settlement in America, but did not reap the profits that it had expected. Even through reorganization and large expenditures, it never achieved its full objective and was increasingly subject to criticism despite its remarkable achievement. The devastating effect of the massacre ushered in a period of attack that never subsided. Commissioners were sent to investigate the Colony at first hand. Charge was met by countercharge and tempers rose high. The Company stubbornly contended for its original charters and James I and Company opponents seemed equally as determined to break them. Matters reached a head in 1624 when James I dissolved the Company, thereby removing the hand that had guided Virginia affairs for 17 years.

With this act Virginia became a royal colony and continued, as such until the American Revolution made it free and independent. From the point of view of the people in the Colony, the change from Company to Crown was almost painless although there was concern over land titles and a continuance of the Assembly. The Company Governor gave way to the royal appointee, but most institutions were left intact. Perhaps a glance at the proceedings of the Assembly of March, 1624 is useful in pointing up the matters of concern to the representatives of the people at this particular time.

At the time Virginia was a going concern. It was well established, economically sound, and expanding at a considerable rate. The business at this session embraced some 35 laws, or acts. Of this total 7 dealt with the economic situation, 8 with Indian affairs and security, 8 with religious matters, 6 with local organization and welfare and 5 with matters of personal and community rights. In the main they suggest growth and an established order.

In the economic sphere there was concern for the planting of ample corn, emphasis on fencing and planting "vines, hearbs, rootes, &c." Commodity rates were in need of further enforcement. It was duly ordered, too, that there would be "no waightes nor measures used, but such as shalbe Sealed by officers Appointed for that purpose."

In matters of safety the chief concern was still the Indian. Trading for corn with the natives was to be prohibited. It was required that "every dwellinge howse shalbe pallizadoed," that guards be maintained and that careful and constant inspection by commanders insure working and ready arms and ammunition. Good watch was to be maintained even when at work in the fields and powder was not to be wasted "unnecessarily in drinking or entertainementes." It was determined that in mid-summer the people of "every corporatione" should fall on the Indians near them "as we did the last yeere" presumably to burn their crops and houses.

Church affairs came in for considerable regulation. One act required that a place be set aside for the worship of God in each and every plantation, a place or "roome sequestred for that purpose" as well as "a place sequestred onlye to the buryall of the dead." A fine, one pound of tobacco for one Sunday but fifty pounds for a month of absences, was imposed for missing the Sunday service. Ministers were exhorted to look after their charges and the people were not to "disparage" their ministers without "sufficient proofe." Payment of the minister's salary was to be insured and there were regulations against "swearinge and drunkennes." A formal order was passed that March 22, the date of the massacre of two years before, be "solemnized as [a] hollidaye." In matters of church conformity the action was specific, "That there be an uniformitie in our Church as neere as may be, to the canons in Englande both in [substance] and circumstance and that all persons yeeld redie obedience unto them under pain of censure."

Government organization and operation was spelled out in a number of instances. To meet the needs of a growing and spreading population special courts were set up for Elizabeth City and Charles City. At least in cases involving no more than 100 pounds of tobacco and for petty offences, it would not be necessary to journey to Jamestown. It was further ordered that all private holdings be duly surveyed, bounded, and recorded. A public "grainary" was ordered to be established in each parish. Control of trade was sought by specifying that no ships should "break boulke [bulk] or make privatt sales of any comodities" before reaching Jamestown. Taxes were not ignored either for a levy of ten pounds of tobacco, already the common currency it appears, was laid on each male above 16 years of age to help defray the "publique depte [debt]." Lest it be forgotten, it was enacted that obedie. e was required "to the presente government."

Old planters were given special exemption from public service, "they and theire posteritie," while Burgesses were rendered exempt from seizure during Assembly time. "Persones of qualitie" when found delinquent, it was stated, could be imprisoned if not fit to take corporal punishment. It is of note that service to

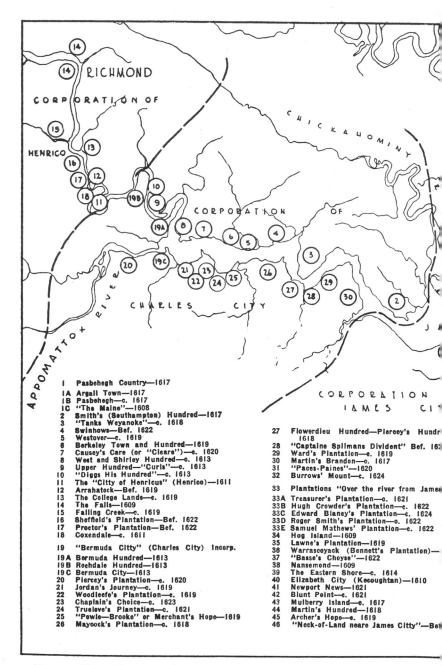

RICHMOND

CORPORATION OF

HENRICO

CHICKAHOMINY

CORPORATION OF

CORPORATION OF CHARLES CITY

APPOMATTOX RIVER

CORPORATION
IAMES CIT

1 Pasbehegh Country—1617
1A Argall Town—1617
1B Pasbehegh—c. 1617
1C "The Maine"—1608
2 Smith's (Southampton) Hundred—1617
3 "Tanks Weyanoke"—c. 1618
4 Swinhows—Bef. 1622
5 Westover—c. 1619
6 Berkeley Town and Hundred—1619
7 Causey's Care (or "Cleare")—c. 1620
8 West and Shirley Hundred—c. 1613
9 Upper Hundred—"Curls"—c. 1613
10 "Diggs His Hundred"—c. 1613
11 The "Citty of Henricus" (Henrico)—1611
12 Arrahatock—Bef. 1619
13 The College Lands—c. 1619
14 The Falls—1609
15 Falling Creek—c. 1619
16 Sheffield's Plantation—Bef. 1622
17 Proctor's Plantation—Bef. 1622
18 Coxendale—c. 1611

19 "Bermuda Citty" (Charles City) Incorp.

19A Bermuda Hundred—1613
19B Rochdale Hundred—1613
19C Bermuda City—1613
20 Piercey's Plantation—c. 1620
21 Jordan's Journey—c. 1619
22 Woodleefe's Plantation—c. 1619
23 Chaplain's Choice—c. 1623
24 Truelove's Plantation—c. 1621
25 "Powle—Brooke" or Merchant's Hope—1619
26 Mayocck's Plantation—c. 1618

27 Flowerdieu Hundred—Piercey's Hundr
1618
28 "Captaine Spilmans Dividend" Bef. 162
29 Ward's Plantation—c. 1619
30 Martin's Brandon—c. 1617
31 "Paces-Paines"—1620
32 Burrows' Mount—c. 1624

33 Plantations "Over the river from James
33A Treasurer's Plantation—c. 1621
33B Hugh Crowder's Plantation—c. 1622
33C Edward Blaney's Plantation—c. 1624
33D Roger Smith's Plantation—c. 1622
33E Samuel Mathews' Plantation—c. 1622
34 Hog Island—1609
35 Lawne's Plantation—1619
36 Warrascoyack (Bennett's Plantation)—
37 "Basse's Choyse"—1622
38 Nansemond—1609
39 The Eastern Shore—c. 1614
40 Elizabeth City (Kecoughtan)—1610
41 Newport News—1621
42 Blunt Point—c. 1621
43 Mulberry Island—c. 1617
44 Martin's Hundred—1618
45 Archer's Hope—c. 1619
46 "Neck-of-Land neare James Citty"—Bef

Towns, Plantations, Settlements and Communities in Virginia: 1607-16

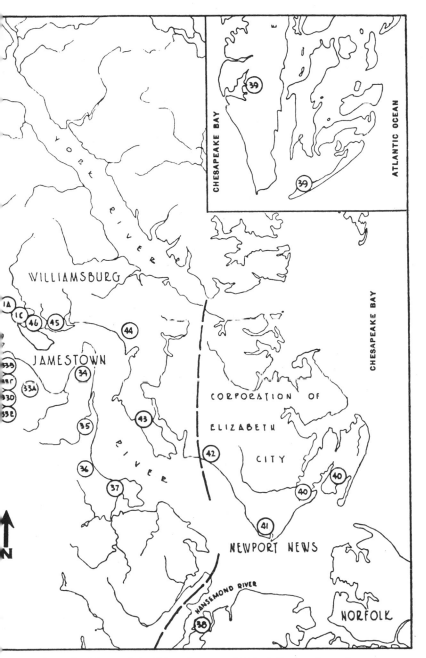

(The sites of Richmond, Williamsburg and Norfolk are shown but
the cities did not exist at the time.)

the Governor, or the public, was made contingent on Assembly consent. Of particular interest, too, was the action on the principle of taxation. It was bold, indeed, at this time for the Assembly to declare that;

The Governor shall not laye any taxes or impositiones uppon the Colony, theire landes or comodities otherwi[se] then by the awthoritie of the Generall Assemblie, to be levied and imployed as the saide Assembly shall appoint.

This was an early word on taxation, but it was to be far from the last word in the next century and a half.

THE SPREAD OF SETTLEMENT—1607 TO 1624

By 1624 the Colony had grown from a single settlement at Jamestown to a series of communities along the James River and on the Eastern Shore. Until 1611 only Jamestown had proven lasting. In this fourth year, however, Kecoughtan (Elizabeth City) was established on a permanent basis and Henrico was laid out. In 1613 the fourth of the Company settlements was established at Bermuda which was to become Charles City. For five years the center of population passed up river. The area in the "Curls" of the James for a time was the preferred location. It looked as if even the seat of goverment would be moved here where much official business was transacted. In 1616 John Rolfe listed 6 settlements and according to his report, some 68 per cent of the residents were in the Henrico-Bermuda area.

Decline set in, in the up-river settlements, however, and the focus returned again to the Jamestown area, aided, it seems, by the efforts of Governor Samuel Argall. It was this 1617-19 period, too, that saw the beginning of particular plantations which did much to populate the James River basin as far as the falls. In 1619 at the time of the Assembly meeting, there were eleven localities, or communities, that sent representatives to Jamestown. Plantations continued to multiply until the destruction of the massacre temporarily rolled back the number. For a time the settlements were reduced to, perhaps, a dozen. Even the massacre, however, could not long hold back what was becoming a tide. The reoccupation of abandoned areas and the utilization of new land was quickly the order of the day. In 1625 a total of 27 areas or communities were reported. In this surge of expansion the center of population now passed again from Jamestown and rested in the lower areas of the James. In 1624 and 1625 Elizabeth City was indeed Virginia's most populous community. In fact, early in 1625 the Elizabeth City group (Kecoughtan, Buckroe, Newport News, etc.) had a greater population than did all of the plantations above Jamestown. At this point "James Citty" and the Island stood second with a population of 175 while Elizabeth City alone had about 350.

The story of Virginia's first seventeen years was written all along the banks of the James and much of it in the towns, forts, and plantations that grew here. Each of them has an individual story and together they give much of the story of Virginia's early years.

PASBEHEGH COUNTRY (1)

The country westward from Jamestown Island along the north shore of the James River as far as the Chickahominy River was known early as Pasbehegh Country from the Indians which inhabited there. Jamestown, as a matter of fact, was considered to have been established in Pasbehegh territory. This area began to feature in the immediate history of Virginia when, in 1608, the colonists elected to build their glass furnaces on the mainland at the top of the isthmus leading to the Island. This, although an unsuccessful enterprise, functioned for a time and people were in residence here. When the enterprise was revived about 1620 the same site, it is thought, was again used. In 1624 it is reported that five persons were then living at the "glase house." Presumably these were associated with the glass project.

The settlement of the general area is not clear as to date. It is stated that Sir Thomas Dale granted "some small parcells" in Pasbehegh, perhaps, as early as 1614. These probably were immediately seated and planted. Samuel Argall returned to Virginia, which he had served well in the 1609-14 days, as governor in 1617. He, likewise, is credited with having granted "some small parcells" here. Argall, too, is identified with the creation of a distinct settlement in the area, one that, for a time, bore his name. This was Argall's Guift, more often mentioned as Argall's Town.

ARGALL TOWN (1A)

Samuel Argall, it seems, was attracted to the area west of Jamestown and established his people here. He and his associates had been assigned 2,400 acres for the transportation of 24 persons by Charter of March 30, 1617 issued just before he left England. This was one of the first such grants. There were settlers with him, too, to be employed on land set aside for the support of the Governor's office. Evidently his settlement, or plantation, got underway in 1617 and two years later was listed among the populated areas in the Colony. It was one of the eleven communities which sent representatives to the First Assembly in 1619. They were Thomas Pawlett and Edward Gourgaing.

To advance the settlement, Argall had contracted for the clearing of some 300 acres of ground (600 pounds sterling it was to cost). This was to be done by colonists assigned to Martin's Hundred. Other arrangements were made with Captain William Powell to clear ground and to erect a house, this to cost £50. This was the Powell whom Argall made the Captain of the Governor's Company and Guard, Lieutenant Governor and Commander of Jamestown, the blockhouses and the people. Evidently Argall and Powell intended to pass on this cost to the "Inhabitants of Paspaheigh, alias Argall's towne" for these people sought "an absolute discharge from certain bondes wherein they stood bound to Captain Samuell Argall for the payment of 600 lb and to Captain William Powell, at Captaine Argall's appointment, for the payment of 50 lb more. To Captaine Argall for 15 skore acres of wooddy ground, called by the name of Argal's towne or Paspaheigh; to Captain Powell in respect of his paines in clearing the grounde and building the houses, for which Captaine Argal ought to have given him satisfaction."

Seemingly the accommodations which resulted were good ones for when, in 1619, some newly arrived Martin's Hundred people were seated here, there was good and convenient housing which enabled them to do the "best of all new-comers." They reaped better crops and the list of those who died was "not comparable to other places." Argall Town, however, was not destined to become a settled community. It was on the Governor's land and Yeardley proceeded after his arrival in 1619 to take a "petty rente" from the settlers here "to make them acknowledge . . . that Paspaheigho by expresse wordes in the greate commission did belonge to the Governor and that they had bene wrongfully seated by Capt. Argall upon that lande."

PASBEHEGH (PASPAHEGH) AND "THE MAINE" (1B-C)

With Yeardley's arrival steps were taken to lay out the 3,000 acres set aside for the Governor's office. This was specified to be on the land "formerly conquered or purchased from the Paspahegh Indians" and included Argall Town. It seemingly was directly east of another 3,000 acres of Company land set aside for the profit of the Company. The Company tract adjoined the Chickahominy River. Both the Company and Governor's land was to be tilled chiefly by tenants. The exact bounds of Pasbehegh, even with these specifications, is difficult to fix. Even landownership in the period prior to 1625 is difficult to define. It seems fairly evident that two communities developed in the area between Powhatan Creek and the Chickahominy, that closest to Jamestown being "the Maine" (mainland). There are references, however, that clearly indicated that both were collectively referred to on occasion as Pasbehegh, as when in 1621 there is mention of the "Subberbs of James Cittie called by the name of Paspehayes," and on occasion as "the Main" as in the listing of residents in 1624. On the other hand, other references are equally as suggestive of two communities. There is separate mention as early as 1619 and a clear differentiation in the census of 1625.

In 1625 there were some 43 people at Pasbehegh including 10 of the Governor's men. Among the total were 7 wives and 3 children. Seemingly the decision to hold this area after the massacre, "James Cittie with Paspehay," took the families back to the land. The settlement, in 1625, seemed well stocked with arms but had no livestock.

Nearby in "the Maine" lived an additional 36 persons of which the largest single muster was that of Thomas Bunn with his wife, son, a maid and four other servants. It was somewhat less well equipped in arms than its neighbor although in most categories it was comparable. Only 3 houses were enumerated yet this was 2 more than given for Pasbehegh. Perhaps, living conditions were deteriorating.

It may be significant that the General Court in January, 1626, reiterated the permission given "to the inhabitants of Pasbehaye to remove themselves from that place." No restraint would be placed on them "nor any other the inhabitants of the Maine to stay and inhabit there." Perhaps, the insecurity of being on the "Governor's Land" was one reason that these "free men" could, and wanted to, leave. The reasons offered, however, were "the barreness of the ground whereon they plant," "the badness of their utterly decayed houses" and "their small strength & ability to hold & defend the same place."

Smith's (Southampton) Hundred (2)

This, along with Martin's Hundred and Argall's settlement, was among the first particular plantations to be established in

Virginia and was founded and promoted by the "Society of Smyth's Hundred." It took its name from Sir Thomas Smith who was treasurer of the Virginia Company and a heavy investor. When he sold his interest in 1620 to his successor, the Earl of Southampton, the designation was changed from Smith's to Southampton Hundred. The initial grant was for some 80,000 acres and it was located on the north shore of the James between the Chickahominy River and the Weyanoke territory.

The first settlers to come over in the venture appear to have arrived in the ship *George* in 1617. In 1618 it was planned to send another 35 and supplies were arranged including "Tooles for a brickyard" and "A mill to grind" tools. The items enumerated can be found in the *Records of the Virginia Company of London* in Volume III, pages 95-96. From a good start it seemingly became, for a time, the leading plantation on the James. When Yeardley arrived as Governor he became interested in this project in which he obviously had a financial stake at least to the extent of bringing "out of England at my chardge 25 men this year [1619] to furnish Smyth hundred . . . ." Yeardley wrote on April 29, 1619, that the plantation was "alltogether destitute of cowes." He asked that more be sent and that authority be sought to purchase as they were available. He hoped to get in the Colony "as many as will sett up 3 ploughs at Smythes Hundred, for we have there great store of good cleered grounds." He was disappointed in not having a good tobacco crop but drought and other things had prevented it. "I cannot expect much tobako our cheifest care must be for corne."

When representatives were chosen for the Assembly in 1619, Capt. Thomas Graves and Walter Shelley went up to Jamestown from Smith's Hundred. Already a church had been founded here. It was St. Marys Church to which Mary Robinson was a benefactor having made possible a communion cup, a plate, a carpet, an altar cloth, "one surplisse" and other ornaments and hangings to the value of twenty pounds. The Society of Smith's

Hundred became interested, too, in the rearing of Indian children in the Christian way when another benefactor assured financial support. It was agreed that arrangements would be found for all not accommodated at Berkeley and Martin's hundreds and elsewhere. This particular plantation was among those to be encouraged by Company and Colony. Products they reaped could be returned to their own adventurers.

Yeardley continued for some time as commander of the hundred. He held court, made land grants, and conducted other Colony business here, perhaps, in "the now mansion house of mee the said George Yeardley in Southampton Hundred." In January, 1620, he advised "not onely the Adventurers for Smythes hundred, but the generall Company also, to send hither husbandmen truly bred (whereof here is a great scarcity, or none at all) both to manage the plough and breake our oxen and horses to that busines." In the same period John Rolfe wrote that the Smith's Hundred people had seen much sickness even though they were seated "at Dauncing Point, the most convenyent place within their lymittes." For this reason "no matter of gaine or greate industry can be expected from them." On the matter of sickness George Thorpe wrote from Southampton Hundred on December 19, 1620 that Virginia was healthy and that he was "perswaded that more doe die here of the disease of theire minde then of theire body by havinge this countrey victualles overpraised unto them in England & by not knowinge they shall drinke water here." He added hopefully, perhaps, that "wee have found a waie to make soe good drinke of Indian corne," that he often preferred it to "good stronge Englishe beare."

Society expenditures continued as forty-two more colonists were sent, of which five died en route in August 1619. Supplies were dispatched, including "English meale" and equipment furnished. The latter, early in 1620, included forty swords and thirty-three suits of armor plus two more "better then ordinary" totaling thirty-two pounds in cost.

The two Smith's Hundred ventures into iron production failed for the same reason that the College project failed. The men "were not able to mannage an iron worke and soe turned good honest tobaccoe mongers." The results of their fishing "in the North Colony," for which they had special "lycence," are less clear. The plantation did have its own shipping. Again, this time early in 1622, they were called on to undertake the education and rearing of some 30 of the "infidelles children," "Children of the Virginians."

The massacre appears to have been the blow that ended the promising hopes of Smith's Hundred. Only 5 persons were slain here but the effects were more far reaching. It was to be one of the settlements to be held and well fortified. In June, 1622, it was reported that "the inhabitants of Southampton Hundred since the late bloudy murthering of [the] nation by the Indians, hath been often infested by them & still is above other plantations wherby they are not onlie putt from planting corne, tobacco, & other nessarie employmentes wherby they might be able to subsist, but also have no corne for the present to maintaine life."

It would appear that the plantation was abandoned and that its survivors may have been relocated at Hog Island where the adventurers had an interest. This was an unfruitful end after the expenditure of some 6,000 pounds sterling. The net result in 1625 was some cattle, "land belonging to Southampton Hundred containeing 100000 acres" and a tract with some tenants on it at Hog Island.

"TANKS WEYANOKE" (3)

About midway along the north shore of the James River between the Chickahominy and Appomattox Rivers is a projection of land that forces a wide sharp turn in the James. The Indians called this Tanks (little) Weyanoke, a place where the river goes around the land. This was separate, and distinct, from Great

Weyanoke which lay along the south side of the James toward the Appomattox. The Weyanoke Indian tribe inhabited both areas, yet their chief town was on the south side.

In 1617 the Indian chieftain Opechancanough, who later would master mind the massacre, presented Sir George Yeardley with a sizeable tract here later described as 2,200 acres. On November 18, 1618, in his instructions, the Company confirmed the Indian grant to Yeardley "in consideration of the long and good and faithful service done by . . . [him] in our said Colony and plantation of Virginia." Two hundred acres were allowed for two shares of stock and 2,000 were allowed for services rendered. Bounds for "Weyanoke," and for adjacent "Konwan" which was also included, were described and it was declared to be in "the territory of the said Charles City."

This was but one of Yeardley's developed properties. He, it seems, put men to work here and sought to open it up and make it profitable. Presumably this was after 1619 yet before 1622. It was mentioned in April, 1619 as a plantation begun in the period beginning in 1617. It seems significant, however, that it had no representation in the Assembly of 1619 unless it be assumed that the Smith's Hundred representatives spoke for it or unless it was grouped with Yeardley's Flowerdieu Hundred across the river.

At the time of the massacre "At Weynoack of Sir George Yeardly his people" some 21, one of whom was Margery Blewet a woman, were slain. With this, the plantation was abandoned and there seems no record of its immediate reoccupation. There is no reason to think that it was ever declared to be a part of Smith's Hundred to the east although Yeardley was fearful of it at one point due principally to the activity of Samuel Argall. The only entry in the land grants list of 1625 is "Tancks Wayonoke over against Perceys Hundred, 2,000 acres." By this date Yeardley had disposed of it through sale to Capt. Abraham Piercey who, also, had purchased Flowerdieu (Piercey's) Hundred.

Swinhows (4)

George Swinhow was an "Adventurer to Virginia" about 1618 to the extent of £37 10s. By 1620 this had increased to £62 10s, and included provisions to the extent of 2 hogsheads and a half ton. He, himself, came to Virginia in the *Diana* and seems to have settled a plantation on the north side of the James in the vicinity of Weyanoke and Westover. This was prior to 1622. When the massacre came on March 22 it left 7 dead "at Mr. Swinhowe his house," Mrs. Swinhow, 2 sons, and 4 others.

There is no record that he returned to his 300 acres in the Corporation of Charles City. In 1625 he was a resident of "the Maine" near Jamestown where he had but one servant with him. Evidently he was a tobacco planter, for when he died, a year later, he left "a hundred gilders which was ten pounde sterlinge for to make the most of his tobacco."

Westover (5)

It appears to have been in the summer of 1619 that Captain Francis West laid out the site of Westover plantation. This was done on the strength of fixing the grant of land in Virginia due Henry, the fourth Lord De La Warr—son and heir of Governor De La Warr who served the Colony for many years. There was some delay, however, in getting a duly authorized patent. On January 10, 1620, when Yeardley wrote of seating the Berkeley Hundred people, he appeared to be concerned lest he be accused of infringing on the West claim. He pointed out that the new settlement was more up river—"more towardes West and Sherley Hundred, and towardes Charles Citty." He went further and stated that West, before his departure for England, did not obtain "any grante" from him as Governor and consequently the bounds of what he did lay out were not known precisely.

There is scanty information relative to the development of Westover. At the time of the Indian massacre, however, it is clear that three Wests, Captain Francis, Captain Nathaniel, and Mr. John, all brothers and each at one time governor of Virginia, were established here. Two persons were killed at each of their plantations, "at Westover, about a mile from Berkley Hundred." In the Assembly of 1624 Westover sent its representative to the Assembly at Jamestown in the person of Samuel Sharpe. This being the case, it is difficult to explain the absence of the plantation from the list of 1624 and the muster of 1625. In the May, 1625 land tabulation, there is a single entry which reads "Att Westover 500 acres claymed by Captaine Francis West." From later events it would appear that the plantation had a continuous history with, perhaps, a small break caused by the massacre.

Berkeley Town and Hundred (6)

In February, 1619, the Virginia Company granted the authority to establish a "particular plantation" in Virginia to a group composed of Richard Berkeley, Sir William Throckmorton, Sir George Yeardley, George Thorpe and John Smyth of Nibley. The initial move toward settlement appears to have been made in the following summer when a ship, the *Margaret*, was fitted out and dispatched with emigrants and supplies. The 35, whose names are known, reached Virginia and on November 30, Ferdinando Yate, one of the group who chronicled the voyage, reported that "in the evening god bethanked we came to anker at Necketan [Kecoughtan] in a good harbore."

It was a little later that the site of the settlement was selected on the north side of the James. Reputed to contain 8,000 acres and 12½ square miles, it was above Westover and "more towards West and Sherley Hundred, and towards Charles Citty." Yeardley elected to describe it thus to emphasize that it did not conflict with any claims of the Wests at Westover. Yate concluded his journal relating "we are well settled in good land by the means of the Governor of this cuntrie." He noted, too, that "our house is built with a stoore convenient." "The people were then following daiely husbantrie, sum to clering ground for corn and tobacko, sum to building houses, sum to plant vines and mulberie trees."

A number of the papers concerned with the initial establishment of Berkeley Hundred survive and at least give an insight into what was intended. The undertaking was expected to reflect "to the honor of allmighty god, the inlargeinge of Christian religion and to the augmentation and renowne of the generall plantation in that cuntry, and the particular good and profit of ourselves, men and servants, as wee hope." There was a very special instruction, perhaps, of some unusual note: "wee ordaine that the day of our ships arrivall at the place assigned for plantation in the land of Virginia shall be yearly and perputualy keept holy as a day of thanksgiving to Almighty god." Was this the first specific Thanksgiving Day in America?

Capt. John Woodleefe was named, and sent, as governor or commander of the new plantation. He, a man of some years of experience in Virginia affairs, was cautioned to keep his and Berkeley Hundred affairs separate and not to seat his own people "unles full ten English miles from . . ." Berkeley. Specific orders were given him relative to building houses which should be "homelike" and "covered wth boardes," some "framed" and to enclosing 400 acres "with a strong pale of seaven foote and halfe highe." Religious conformity and practice was stressed. All was to be "observed and kept, according as it is used in the Church of England."

There was soon a change in direction as a new charter placed the management of affairs in Virginia directly in the hands of George Thorpe and of William Tracy who was assigned Throckmorton's interest in the project. Thorpe left for the Colony in the spring of 1620 and with him went 3 men and "six kyne." A larger reinforcement accompanied Tracy. It included 50 persons who left England in the fall of 1620 reaching Virginia on January 29, 1621. Tracy wrote in September that he had in his Company "4 maid servants 3 maried wives & 2 young children my wife and daughter & son." The full list of supplies that came at this time is preserved (*Records of the Virginia Company of London*, III, 385-393) and tells much of life and conditions in Virginia. It included 2 grindstones, 2 mill stones, garden seeds: parsnips, carrot, cabbage, turnip, lettuce, onion, mustard and garlic; books on "husbandry & huswifry;" 22,500 "nayles of severall sorts;" and "sives to make gunpowder in Virginia." (*See the Appendix.*)

Things were well advanced when the massacre hit Berkeley Hundred. Eleven were killed here including Capt. George Thorpe "one of his Majesties pensioners." Then came abandonment from which no clearcut survival seems to have been achieved. In the spring of 1622 those who "remayneth" must have been relocated. Four persons sent from England "before the news of the massacre was heard" arrived in June and there is mention of others going for Berkeley in August. In July, 1623 John Smith promised to supply "my servants now living in Virginia in Berckley Hundreth" and others at least to the extent of £100. Two months later the *Bonny Bess* is reported to have brought people and supplies for Berkeley in its cargo.

In January, 1624, it was reported that 16 men, all of whom are named, were "planted at Sherley Hundred for Barkley Hundred Company." This indicates that the settlement at Berkeley had not yet been reactivated. Further indication is found in the assignment of Richard Milton of "Shirley Hundred" to look after the "Barkley Hundred" cattle for which he would get 50 pounds of tobacco and "the milke of the said Kyne." Perhaps these are the same cattle which had been taken to Jordan's Journey, by overseer Kemish, just after the massacre. There is no mention of Berkeley in the list of 1624, or in the muster of 1625.

CAUSEY'S CARE (OR "CLEARE") (7)

Nathaniel Causey was an old soldier who came to Virginia in the First Supply early in 1608. It was on December 10, 1620 that he obtained a grant that he began to develop as a private plantation. This appears to have been located just to the east of West and Shirley Hundred on the north side of the James. If we accept the entry in the land list of May, 1625 this was for some 200 acres. Presumably he and his wife, Thomasine, also an "old planter" who had come to the Colony in 1609, lived here, at least for a time, perhaps, with servants which numbered 5 in 1625.

In the massacre Causey "being cruelly wounded, and the salvages about him, with an axe did cleave one of their heads, whereby the rest fled and he escaped." In 1624 Causey, who sat in the Assembly, is thought to have represented Jordan's Journey where he is listed as in residence that same year and again in 1625. He was among the 31 who signed the Assembly's reply to the declaration of charges against the Smith administration of the Colony made by Alderman Johnson and others. His plantation, Causey's Care, across the river from Jordan's Journey, continued, it seems, and for years was a landmark of the vicinity. Causey appears occasionally in the court records as when on May 23, 1625, he assumed a debt and obligation to "Doctor Pott" which required the delivery of "one barrel of Indian corne" to "James Cittie at the first cominge downe of the next boate."

WEST AND SHIRLEY HUNDRED (8)

This plantation, or hundred, on the north side of the James across from the mouth of the Appomattox River first comes into view as one of the areas in the Bermuda Incorporation established by Dale. Settlement is thought to date from 1613. As time passed it appears to have developed with less restrictive ties to Bermuda City than the hundreds adjoining it on the south side of the river. There is little to indicate that Bermuda Hundreds' claim on it in 1617 was ever seriously considered.

There is a glimpse of life here in Ralph Hamor's, *A True Discourse of the Present Estate of Virginia*: "At West and Sherley Hundred, (seated on the North side the river lower then the

Bermuda 3 or 4 myles) are 25 commaunded by Captaine [Isaac] Maddeson who are imployed only in planting and curing tobacco, with the profitt thereof to cloth themselves, and all those who labor about the generall busynes." As such it was one of 6 settlements in Virginia, fourth in point of population.

It continued to develop as a rather important community. Even though not listed as sending representatives to Jamestown in 1619, it probably shared the services of the Burgesses entered from Charles City. It was listed as an established settlement when Argall left the Colony in April, 1619. Its name in the first decade fluctuated considerably first appearing as "Wests Sherly Hundred" then becoming "West and Sherly" and then Sherley (or Shirley).

The list of those killed in the massacre has no entry specifically labeled for this plantation indicating, perhaps, that the effect here was light. This may explain why it was one of the few points designated to be held after March 22, 1622, much the most interior, or westward point on the north side of the James. In 1624 "West and Sherlow Hundred" had its own Burgesses in the Assembly in the persons of Isaac Madison and Richard Biggs. In 1623 a special appointment had been made to Grivell Pooley, to make a special levy at "Sherley Hundred" and adjacent plantations. This, being 10 pounds of tobacco and 1 bushel of corn "for every planter and tradesman above the age of sixteene yeares alive at the cropp" time, was to meet the Corporation's yearly minister's salary and to aid in "publique charges."

In 1624 a total of 69 inhabitants were listed for Shirley Hundred, 45 in the Hundred and 24 "at West and Sherlow hundred Island." Perhaps this included the 16 persons who had been "planted at Sherley Hundred for Barkley Hundred Company." A year later the population stood at 61 with the decrease evidently all registered at the "Island." At this time there were 17 houses, 2 boats and ample corn and fish and some peas. There were 21 head of cattle, 24 hogs and 263 items of poultry. Small arms (47) and armor (31) seemed adequate although Indians still infested the place and occasionally a man was killed. Land grants listed in May, 1625 totaled 36 (4,410 acres) but of these only 8 (1,150 acres) were given as "planted." The majority of the holdings were 100 acres or less and there were 3,000 acres of Company land below "Sherley Hundred Island."

Upper Hundred—"Curls" (9)

This area, on the north side of the James below Henrico and across from Bermuda (Nether) Hundred, was one of the several hundreds annexed to, or included in, the corporation of Bermuda City. Settlement seems to have begun in 1613 although little is known of events in the early years. "Curls" evidently was a name suggested by the course of the river here. The reported patent for 400 acres to Edward Gurgany in October, 1617 has been assumed to have been in this area. In 1619 Gurgany's widow bequeathed the tract to Capt. Thomas Harris. Progress in the occupation and use of the ground was severely checked by the massacre.

"Diggs His Hundred" (10)

This was a plantation, one of several, that Dale annexed to the new Bermuda City incorporation in 1613. In this it was similar to Bermuda Upper Hundred being on the north side of the river and adjoining it, perhaps, on the west. Neither of these hundreds seems to have had the closely integrated relationship with Bermuda City that the Bermuda Nether and Rochdale hundreds had. Settlement, however, seems to date from this early period even though little is known of it. An assignment of 100 acres of land to Samuel Jordan in July, 1622 clearly establishes that there was continuing activity at Diggs. This tract in "Diggs His Hundred" had earlier been owned by one Mary Tue. This transaction, shortly after the massacre certainly demonstrates that, although the Indian slaughter caused evacuation here, interest in reoccupation quickly revived.

49

In the late summer of 1611 Sir Thomas Dale departed Jamestown with a strong force of 300 men to proceed up river to establish a new settlement. It was expected that it would become the chief seat in the Colony. It would be further removed from the Spanish fear and threat, it would be more healthful, and it could be made more defensible against the Indians.

The Company and many of the settlers were dissatisfied with the Jamestown location. Dale had begun to push this project soon after his arrival in the Colony in May, 1611. He was acting on conviction and on Company instructions. Seemingly the name of the new town had already been chosen. It was to be Henrico in honor of Henry, Prince of Wales, known too as the protector and patron of Virginia. He had explored and found the site he liked, "a convenient strong, healthie and sweete seate to plant a new Towne in." Already at Jamestown he had prepared "pales, posts and railes to impaile his proposed new Towne."

Marshal Dale, leaving Governor Gates at Jamestown, proceeded upstream by boat while the larger part of his party went overland led by Capt. Edward Brewster. The latter encountered resistance from the Indians particularly at the hand of "Munetute" ("called amongste us Jacke of the feathers"). Dale and Brewster rendezvoused at the appointed place and "after divers encounter and skirmishes with the salvages gained a convenientt place for fortification where presently they did begin to builde a foarte." The Indians continued to protest this invasion of their territory with the most effective means at hand. The site selected was a peninsula that jutted into the James from the north side some few miles below the Arrahatock village.

Within 15 days Dale had impaled 7 acres of ground and then set to work to build at each of the 5 corners of the town "very strong and high commanders or watchtowers, a faire and handsome Church, and storehouses." It was not until then that he turned to the matter of houses and lodgings for "himself and men." Two miles inland he built a strong pale some 2 miles in length which ran from river to river making an island of the neck on which Henrico stood. Presumably this palisade faced a ditch hence the term—"trench and pallizado." Hamor related in 1614 that in 4 months he had made Henrico "much better and of more worth then all the work ever since the Colonie began."

His achievements were not come by easily. It was costly in life and in loss of personal freedoms. It was achieved with the full enforcement of the now famous "Dale laws." He moved quickly to punish deserters and law breakers. George Percy related the results in graphic terms. Some "in a moste severe manner [he] cawsed to be executed. Some he appointed to be hanged, some burned, some to be broken upon wheles, others to be staked and some to be shott to deathe; all theis extreme and crewell tortures he used and inflicted upon them to terrefy the reste for attemptinge the like. . . ." These were stern measures that produced results and few of his contemporary associates took issue including John Rolfe, Ralph Hamor, Reverend Alexander Whitaker and even Sir Edwin Sandys. To them, motivated by the spirit of the time, hard conditions required stern handling.

Robert Johnson, in 1612, evaluated the new settlement as he saw it: "the colony is removed up the river forescore miles further beyond Jamestown to a place of high ground, strong and defensible by nature, a good air, wholesome and clear, unlike the marshy seat at Jamestown, with fresh and plenty of water springs, much fair and open grounds freed from woods, and wood enough at hand." In 1614 Hamor described the town here as having "3 streets of well framed howses, a hansom Church, and the foundations of a more stately one laid, of brick, in length one hundred foote, and fifty foot wide, beside store houses, watch houses, and such like." Near it, and behind the pale, was a great quantity of corn ground—enough to support the whole Colony and easy for "manuring and husbandry."

Two years later it seems evident that the "citty of Henricus" had retrogressed, perhaps, out of emphasis on Bermuda City just down river. At this time there were only 38 men and boys "at *Henrico* and in the precints." Of these 22 were "Farmors," the rest were "Officers and others." Although it was "our furthest habitacion into the land" it was listed as self sufficient in "food and apparell." Captain Smalley, in the absence of James Davis, was in command and the minister was William Wickham. Wickham "in his life and doctrine gives good examples, and godlie instructions to the people."

Even though the "citty" continued its decline, the Incorporation, of which it was the center, carried on its name. In 1619 Henrico was reported to have had but a few "old" houses, and a "ruinated" Church with some other buildings "in the Island." It continued, however, as a fixed community until destroyed by the Indians during, and after, the massacre. On March 22, 1622 only 5 were killed at "Henrico Iland." It was represented in the assembly of 1619 by John Polentine and Thomas Dowse. The latter may have been actually living on the College land, above the "citty," where he had earlier received a patent from the hand of Argall. There is no mention of Henrico town in 1624 and 1625. As a matter of fact, the only settlement in the entire Incorporation of Henrico listed in the census of 1625 was the College Land. This had been the only community, too, to send representatives to the Assembly in 1624. The effects of the massacre in this area had been great.

ARRAHATOCK (12)

When the settlers first reached Virginia the Arrahatock Indian village appears to have been located several miles above the point where Henrico City was established in 1611. It was, perhaps, near "Arahatec's Joy" where the exploring colonists were feasted on June 2, 1607. This was on the north side of the river which they called the Popham side after Chief Justice Popham. When

Dale laid out his town of "Henricus," it was described as "near to an Indian Towne called Arasahattocke."

At some point in the story, the Indians left, or were driven out of, their town site which was appropriated by the colonists. Even though it was close to, and appears to have been grouped often with the Henrico settlement, it seems, too, to have been a separate and distinct community. At Argall's departure in the spring of 1619, it was listed as one of seven Virginia settlements with Henrico being another. When Yeardley arrived just a little later both Arrahatock and Henrico were listed among the forts, towns and plantations which he found.

In the Assembly of 1619 Thomas Dowse and John Polentine represented the "citty of Henricus" and must have spoken for Arrahatock as well. The site appears to have been included in the College lands a fact that was protested by William Weldon the Commander of the men who settled this property. At the time, late 1619 and early 1620, Capt. Samuel Mathews was established at "Harrowatox" on an excellent site where he had at least two surplus houses. Weldon, with a small complement of his college tenants, was assigned to be "in consortship with Captaine Mathewes" for security and other purposes.

There is some reason to think that the settlement of Arrahatock ("harichatox" or "harry hattocks") reappeared after the massacre. At least its identity as a place name continued for a time.

The College Lands (13)

In the property listing for Virginia made in May, 1625, there is an entry that reads: "On the northerly side of James River, from the Falles downe to Henerico containing about x miles in length, are the publique land's, reserved & laid out, wherof 10,-000 acres, for the Universitie lands, 3000 Acres for the Companys lands, with other land belonging to the Colledge; the common land for the Corporation [of Henrico] 1500 acres." The University and College lands were a testimony to the interest, the efforts, and the work of the Company in behalf of the Christianization of the Indians and the advancement of education in Virginia. The enterprise did not materialize, yet there had been every expectation that it would.

Concentrated attention on the proposed University and, particularly, the College began in 1619 although there is evidence that Argall, when Governor, did some work in this direction. Specific evidence of interest toward Christianizing the Indians and educating the "infidels children" in Virginia is easy to find in the literature and records of the period. Yeardley's instructions in 1618 carried the order to locate a suitable place for a university in the Henrico area. He was to make immediate preparation for building a college there. A generous contribution had already been made in England towards the "planting of a college" and 10,000 acres were to be set aside as an endowment.

When the bishop's collection for the college had reached £1,500, a decision was made. Rather than start construction with too little, it was resolved to send fifty "tenants-at-halves" to work on the land. Half of their income would go to the college project and half to themselves. Profits, it was expected, would augment the building and maintenance fund and help to support tutors and students. In the meanwhile, friendly relations with the Indians were important to make possible the willing education of their children.

The tenants reached Virginia in November, 1619, under the command of William Weldon. Being poorly supplied, however, and inexperienced, the Governor dispersed 30 of them among the old planters and sent Weldon and the remainder to be with Capt. Samuel Mathews at Arrahatock which was actually within the College lands. This was a poor beginning and meant that little would happen within a year. Weldon thought the land to be excellent; "a goodly heritage beinge as pleasant & fruitfull a soile as any this land yeeldeth." It troubled him, however, that two of the best locations were already claimed and planted: one by

Mathews, "for the use of Sir Thomas Midleton & Alderman Johnson," and one by Thomas Dowse. Both were by virtue of grants from Argall. He knew, too, that he needed more men and more supplies. In the meanwhile Virginia's first assembly had endorsed the idea of the "University and Colledge" and asked that it be pushed to fulfillment.

In England, the early beginnings were seen not to have been too successful and the Company committee set up for the purpose explored various possibilities. In the spring of 1620, George Thorpe, a gentleman of the King's privy chamber and a member of the Company Council, was made deputy for the Company to prosecute the project. Already he had gone to Virginia in the interest of Berkeley Hundred. Previously, it appears, an additional fifty tenants had been dispatched to the Colony.

In the meanwhile, much Company effort was diverted to the East India School. This free school, planned to have dependence on Henrico College, was projected for Charles City. Although emphasis was on the education of the Indian, it seems clear that the colonists' children were likewise a consideration. There is specific comment on this as it related to the East India School.

Donations in money and kind such as books and communion service continued to be forthcoming in England. An audit of the Company books early in 1622 showed college receipts to the extent of £2,043 and expenditures of £1,477. In Virginia, George Thorpe continued to encourage peace and friendship with the Indians setting an excellent personal example in this. He did what he could, too, to develop the College lands even planting vines to the number of 10,000.

Then came the massacre which took George Thorpe and 17 of the "Colledge People" located about 2 miles above "Henrico-Citie." The college project did not survive this blow even though the Company urged it and the 60 surviving tenants were returned to the land in the spring of 1623 with the hope of building houses and planting orchards and gardens. Brickmakers were held to their contract against the time when the erection of the "fabricke of the colledge" would be possible.

In 1624, there were 29 persons living on the college lands, and, according to the census of 1625, this had dropped to 22 who were living in 8 houses. They were then deficient in food, excepting fish, and in livestock and were not too well armed, having but 16 armors, 6 swords, and 18 fixed pieces. The excursion into ironmaking had failed after the expenditure of "the greatest parte of the stock belonginge to the Colledge." With the dissolution of the Company the spark for the project seemed gone. One student of this subject, Robert Hunt Land, has concluded: "Possibly a greater blow to Henrico College than the massacre was the revocation of the charter of the Virginia Company of London."

The Falls (14)

One of President Wingfield's first acts in May, 1607, after the construction of James Fort was underway, was the dispatch of a party to explore the river above Jamestown. Twenty-two men under Capt. Christopher Newport left on May 21 and proceeded inland to the falls of the James.

in six dayes they arrived at a [Indian] Towne called Powhatan, consisting of some twelve houses, pleasantly seated on a hill; before it three fertile Iles, about it many of their cornefields, the place is very pleasant, and strong by nature . . . To this place the river is navigable: but higher within a mile, by reason of the rockes and isles, there is not passage for a small boat, this they call the Falles.

Newport's shallop could go no further. Then, as reported, "upon one of the little iletts at the mouth of the falls . . . [Newport] sett up a crosse with this inscription *Jacobus Rex. 1607.* and his owne name below: At the erecting hereof we prayed for our king and our owne prosperous succes in this his action, and proclaimed him king, with a greate showte."

And so it was for more than two years. It was in the late summer of 1609 that Smith sent Capt. Francis West out from Jamestown to establish a settlement at the Falls. He left with 140 men and a six months food supply "to inhabitt there." He secured a site that proved too low in elevation being subject to inundation in times of high water. When Smith went up to look over the new post, he negotiated with the Indians to take over their fortified settlement on a point of high ground. This included lodgings and "300 acres of ground readie to plant," a place which Smith called "Nonsuch."

The shift of site was made in West's absence and when he returned he was not happy with the situation. He preferred the site of his choice and the settlers returned again "to the open aire of West Fort," abandoning "Nonsuch." Indian attack followed and the settlement became untenable. In the fall West returned with his men to Jamestown having lost a goodly number at the "Falles" as well as eleven men and a boat at "Arsetocke" a few miles downstream. One more settlement had temporarily failed.

Lord De La Warr attempted to re-establish the post here in 1610 and built "Laware's Fort" from which he planned to search for minerals in the coming spring. This, too, failed when illness caused him to return to Jamestown, the same sickness, perhaps, that led him to quit Virginia a little later.

FALLING CREEK (15)

In 1619 the Company sent 150 persons to Virginia "to set up three iron works" in view of the fact of "proofe having been made of the extraordinary goodnesse of that iron." This was further manifestation of the continuing interest in Virginia resources, particularly iron. This apparently led to the establishment at Falling Creek of the first regular ironworks within the Colony.

These workmen, equipped "with all Materials and other provisions therunto belonging," were under the direction, care, and charge of a Captain Bluett (Blewet) with whom the Company had contracted. His death, along with that of the "principall officers and cheife men," created some confusion. Yeardley promised to do what he could with this company since he had found "an excellent water and good oare." The lack of "good understanding workers" was, however, serious. In June, 1620, John Pory reported on the "Iron workes" which were "so much affected by the Company." His logic seemed good when he deplored the lack of initial "deliberation there in England." A more careful survey in the Colony by a skilled leader would have been helpful, too, even though "abundant iron . . . and fit places to make it in" had been partially scouted. This comment was made despite the 110 Warwickshire and Staffordshire and the forty Sussex workmen, described as "all framed to iron works," who had been contracted for the project.

It was reported a year later that "the iron workes goeth forward veary well." Another contemporary commented on the works and spoke of "having already receaved a good proofe thereof by iron sent from there." This might have been small comfort for the £4,000 which had been spent already.

In May, 1621, realizing that a replacement for Bluett was needed, the Company entered into an agreement with John Berkeley, "sometimes of Beverstone Castle in the County of Glocester (a gentleman of honourable familie)," as "Master & over-seer" of the works at the site "called The falling Creeke." He agreed to take himself, his son Maurice, three servants from his "private family" and twenty workmen. These would include eight for the furnace (two founders, two keepers, two filers and two carpenters) and twelve others (four finers, two servants, two "chaffery men," two "hammer men" and two servants). He would get £30 toward furnishing his personal group, plus their transportation, and £20 to cover the assembly of the workmen. The twenty workmen, to be bound for seven years of service to the Company, would be transported and "victualled as other tenantes for one whole yeare at the Companies charge."

Letters were dispatched to the Colony urging special care and attention for this new company made up of Berkeley and "his ging." Berkeley evidently felt that the Falling Creek site was ideal "for wood, water, mines and stone." His letters indicated that he expected to be producing good quantities of iron by the late spring of 1622. He envisioned much more for the now £5,000 investment than the disparagingly reported return of a "fire shovell and tonges and a little barre of iron made by a bloomery. . . ." He, however, did not expect the massacre.

The Indians swept down on the ironworks community and left twenty-seven dead as well as considerable destruction to the works. The dead included John Berkeley, a mason, two wives, three children and "Joseph Fitch Apothecary to Doctor Pots." This was the end of the project although the Company demonstrated, for a time, its intention to resume this work which was considered basic for the Colony's welfare. The Virginia Governor and Council would have reinforced the survivors, they reported, if "soe many of the principall worke men had not beene slaine." It was the opinion of Maurice Berkeley, who succeeded his father in command, that "it was utterlie impossible to proceede in that Worke. . . ." Even though, in 1623, it is recorded that the Company sent 9 more men there is nothing to indicate that production was resumed on the 100 acres along Falling Creek that John Blower had "Surrendred for the use of the Iron Works." Another industrial scheme had failed and the Company had taken yet another loss.

SHEFFIELD'S PLANTATION (16)

It appears that sometime prior to March, 1622, Thomas Sheffield obtained a patent for 150 acres located "some three miles from Falling Creeke" and about two miles above "Henrico Iland." He proceeded to establish a settlement here in the Corporation of Henrico. Seemingly all went well until the massacre when the Indians wiped out this advance post on the James. "Master Thomas Sheffeild and Rachel his wife" along with eleven others, including two boys, were slain. There is no mention of further activity at this date.

PROCTOR'S PLANTATION (17)

John Proctor was among those who came to Virginia under a Company Charter in the 1609-15 period. It would appear that he located a plantation well up the James River, on its south side, but below Falling Creek. The land list of 1625 specified that he had a 200 acre grant in this vicinity. Perhaps, he was established here well before the massacre. When the Indians descended on his place, he must have been away, for his wife stood her ground as she did later when the Colony officials sought to force her to vacate the now isolated post. It is reported that "Mistress Proctor, a proper, civill, modest gentlewoman . . . ["fortified and lived in despite of the enemy"] till perforce the English officers forced her and all them with her to goe with them, or they would fire her house themselves, as the salvages did when they were gone. . . ."

In 1624 Proctor and his wife were living "Over the River" from Jamestown and a year later he, his wife Alice and three servants were at Paces Paines. It is not known whether he returned to his plantation upriver from which he had been uprooted in 1622. He had, in 1623, received a patent to transport fifty persons to Virginia together with sufficient necessities and provisions for cultivating the land. The latter seemingly included "a wherry or small boate." There is evidence, too, that he could punish his servants if the occasion warranted even to the extent of using a "line or whip corde."

COXENDALE (18)

Sir Thomas Dale had a good eye for land and security. Consequently he viewed the ground across the James from, and to the west of, Henrico with considerable interest which he translated into action soon after getting his principal settlement under-

60

way in 1611. Here, for the enlargement of the town, some 12 acres were impaled "especially for our hoggs to feed in." He named this locality "Hope in faith, Coxen-dale" and proceeded to secure it with a series of forts which he named Charity, Elizabeth, Patience and Mount Malado. There was "a retreat or guest house" for sick people which was declared to be on "a high seat" with "wholesome air." It was in this area that the Rev. Alexander Whitaker chose his "Parsonage, or church land." This was "som[e] hundred acres impaled, and a faire framed parsonage house built thereupon, called Rocke Hall of this Towne." Capt. James Davis was made commander of the forts.

Coxendale continued to exist and grow, perhaps, despite the inadequacy of the records that relate the story. Rolfe, in 1616, did not list it, yet possibly he considered it to be a part of Henrico. It was listed as one of 9 forts, plantations and towns found in Virginia when Yeardley reached the colony in April, 1619. There is no special reference to it in the list of burgesses named in 1619. Here again it may have been included with Henrico in matters of representation. In matters of land grants, however, it had a separate identity. In the spring of 1619 a grant of 100 acres "Scituate in Coxendale over against the Iland of Henricus" was made to Thomas Read "under the Collonies seale." This was in reward for eight years of "good service in that country." Three years later Read made over this tract, a part of it called "Mount my Lady" to Edward Hurd, a "London cittizen and iron monger."

The massacre struck here, too, as it did elsewhere. The statistics would indicate that the slaughter in this general area was light compared with many other points. Perhaps the water barrier in the "curls" of the river plus the palisades and forts gave greater security. Despite this, when the massacre was over, these points were isolated and removal was ordered. Capt. Roger Smith, on April 20, 1622, was given "absolute power and command in matters of warr, over all the people both in Henerico Ileand and Coxendale . . . uppon paine of death." He was "to use all care and vigilancie" in "the safe bringeing away of all the said people, and cattell, and goodes. . . ."

This was but a temporary delay in settlement as the urge for land and property became greater. Just how soon there was a return here is unclear. In May, 1625, however, 8 patents were listed for Coxendale in the Corporation of Henrico. This was for a total of 802 acres ranging from a twelve acre grant to Lt. Edward Berkeley, to 200 acres to John Laydon. It may be significant that none were marked as "planted."

"Bermuda Citty" (Charles City) Incorporation (19)

In 1612 Marshal Thomas Dale drove the Indians from their habitation about the "curls" of the James and the Appomattox, the river that bears their name. Seeing it to be good ground, he determined to possess it and to establish a settlement here. As Ralph Hamor relates: "I proceed to our next and most hopefull habitation, whether we respect commodity, or security (which we principally aime at) against forraigne designes, and invasions, I meane the Bermuda Citty, begun about Christmas last [1613]. . . ." The initial settlement was near the Appomattox, on its west side, some five miles from Henrico but 14 by the circuitous river route.

Dale was very hopeful of the "new Bermudas" and proceeded to annex "to the freedom, and corporation . . . many miles of champion, and woodland, in several Hundreds" on both sides of the James. These Hamor enumerated as the "[1] Upper and [2] Nether Hundreds, [3] Rochdale Hundred [4] Wests Sherley Hundred, and [5] Diggs his Hundred." Evidently a settlement was begun in each of these areas all of which kept active till the massacre.

Bermuda Hundred (19A)

It was in the Nether Hundred, which became Bermuda Hundred and later the "Neck-of-Land" in Charles City, that settlement was first initiated "for there [according to Hamor in 1614] lyeth the most convenient quantity of corne ground." With a "pale" from river to river but two miles in length it was possible to secure some eight miles of "exceeding good corne ground." Houses were built one-half mile from each other on "the verge of the river." In 1614 these were described as "faire houses, already builded." There were others as well totaling "not so few as fifty." Gates' lieutenant, George Yeardley, was then in charge.

ROCHDALE HUNDRED (19B)

This plantation, just west of Nether (Bermuda) Hundred, was gotten underway about the same time. A "crosse pale," about four miles long, was, in 1614, already built "with bordering houses along the pale." It was in this Hundred that the "hogges, and other cattell" had a 20 mile circuit in which to graze securely.

BERMUDA CITY (19C)

The "chiefe Citty," when Hamor left, was not yet ready. Its construction, at a point across the Appomattox from Bermuda Hundred, while begun, was not pushed until the fall of 1614. Here Bermuda City was fashioned to be "an impregnable retreat, against any forraign invasion, how powerfull so ever." This became the fourth and last of the public, or general, corporations taking its place with James City, Kecoughtan, and Henrico. Within a few years its name would change from Bermuda to Charles City to honor Prince Charles as Henrico had been named for Prince Henry his brother, both being royal sons. Hamor, in 1614, spoke of "Bermuda Citty," evidently meaning to include Bermuda Hundred as well, as "a business of greatest hope, ever begunne in our territories their." At the same time he mentions the special "pattent," or agreement, made between Dale and the people there, "termes and conditions they voluntarily have undertaken."

When Dale assigned small parcels of ground to planters for

their own use prior to, or in, 1613, he did much for the Colony. It stopped some of the drain on the common "magazine" and allowed room for individual profit and enterprise. It also freed the colonists from Company service except in emergencies and for one month a year. In making this arrangement, however, he excepted the Bermuda Incorporation people with whom he made a special contract. They were bound to three years of almost continuous public service in the Bermuda City project "before they have their freedom." At the end of their term, however, they claimed their rights of freedom and the Governor, then Samuel Argall, could not deny their claim. On November 30, 1617, he reported in reply to the "citizens of Bermuda hund[red]" that he would "not infringe their rights being a member of that City himself" but begged that the Colony servants "may stay their this year." Evidently these Bermuda people began to enjoy the rights and freedoms that did not become general until the Company division and "Greate Charter" which evolved in 1618 and 1619.

The center of gravity in the Colony in the 1611-16 period was upriver in the Henrico and Bermuda City area. In Rolfe's report of 1616 "Bermuda Nether Hundred" was by far the most active and most heavily populated area. Its 119 people was much in excess of the 50 at Jamestown which stood second among the 6 populated points. Bermuda's population then embraced chiefly the members of the Corporation although there were 17 "farm-ors" and a few "who labor generally for the Colony, amongst whom, some make pitch and Tarr, Pott-ashes, Chark-coale, and other workes, and are maintayned by the magazin, but are not of the Corporation." Capt. George Yeardley, who was deputy governor and deputy marshal, "for the most part" lived here as did Alexander Whitaker who had the "ministerall chardge."

The "Cities of Henrico & Charles [Bermuda]" were the best fortified points in the Colony standing "upon high ground the cliffes beinge steepe but of a claye mould the ayre good and wholesome." Also "about those places [there were] good quantities of cleared groundes." Fortifications were by "trench and pallizado" with "great timber" blockhouses athwart "passages and for scouring the pallizadoes." There, too, was "access to shipping." Much official business was transacted here where the Governor was in residence much of the time. Courts, on occasion, convened here and official proclamations and documents were issued from the hand of various governors and from the pen of the Colony's secretary. Such was the commission to William Cradock made "provost marshall of Bermuda City and of all the Hundred thereto belonging" from Samuel Argall "Admirall and for the time present principal Governor of Virginia" issued at "Bermuda City" on February 20, 1618 over John Rolfe's signature as "Secretary and Recorder."

It appears to have been Argall that did much to return the emphasis to Jamestown and away from Bermuda. In 1617 he wrote that he preferred Jamestown and proposed to strengthen it as a good healthy site. Charles City remained active, however, and the largest seat in the Colony. In 1619 Samuel Sharpe and Samuel Jordan represented the Bermuda area in the Assembly. It is not known whether they voted for the measure that required all persons from Charles City and other points who were going down river below the Capital to touch "first here at James Citty to knowe whether the Governor will command him any service." By this time Bermuda Hundred and Bermuda City were most often designated "Charles City and Hundred."

It was in 1621 that the Company undertook to establish and build the East India School and to locate this "free schoole in Virginia" at Charles City. A grant of 1,000 acres was set aside and a few workmen were sent to the Colony. For a time it looked as if this center to encourage the "rudiments of learning" and "principles of Religion, civility of life, and humane learning" would materialize. It did not, however, survive the massacre. When the workmen reached Virginia, they were placed among

65

the College tenants and later transferred to Martin's Hundred.

The massacre of 1622 appeared to have been devastating in the Bermuda area and led to its temporary abandonment. The list of those killed is, however, rather light in comparison with settlements such as Martin's Hundred. There were twenty-seven at four specified points. It leads one to doubt that a full list of names was submitted.

Thought soon turned to a repair of the damages. It was judged "very necessarie to raise new workes especiallie at Henrico & Charles Citty" which according to one report were "utterlie demolished by the Indians." This destruction, at least some of it, followed the abandonment of the posts. Houses were burned and "poultry, hoggs, cowes, goates, and horses" were killed in number "to the greate griefe as well as ruine of the olde inhabitants. . . ."

There was a return to the land in some large measure after the massacre. In 1624 a list of 41 residents was given for "the Neck of Land" in Charles City Corporation and the census of 1625 showed 44 in this old Bermuda Hundred area. In 1624 Luke Boys and Thomas Harris sat in the Assembly at Jamestown and may have helped to enact the measure that required "courtes [to be] kept once a moneth in the Corporations of Charles Cittie & Elizabeth Cittie" to handle cases involving petty offenses and sums up to 100 pounds of tobacco. The muster of January 24, 1625 shows the "Neck-of-Land" to have been very well established. Its 44 people had 16 houses and good supplies of corn, fish, livestock, poultry and arms. In May, 1625, ten individual grants (ranging from 50 to 1,150 acres and totaling 2,900) were listed as located here in addition to the corporation and common land.

Piercey's Plantation (20)

At the time of the massacre Abraham Piercey had a plantation adjacent to the Appomattox River and, perhaps, somewhat upstream from the James. Here "at Master Abraham Pierse his plantation some five miles off the Colledge people" four persons, 3 men and a boy were killed. Piercey, a prominent merchant, named to the Council in 1624, may have laid out his acres here, "in lieu of his Long service done the Company," as early as 1620. The holding, in May, 1625, was defined as 1,150 acres obtained by patent. A place name here "Peircies Toyle" Creek very likely is a result of his activity in this area.

JORDAN'S JOURNEY (21)

This plantation took its name from its founder, Capt. Samuel Jordan and appears to have embraced 450 acres. At least in 1625 Jordan was credited with this amount as being "planted" by patent in "the territory of greate Weyanoke." It has been said that he established Jordan's Journey, also known as Beggar's Bush, in 1619 although in the Assembly of 1619 he represented "Charles Citty." He was one of the Assembly Committee of four appointed to examine "the first booke of the fower" of the "Greate Charter." In 1622 Jordan received a share of Company stock from Mary Tue as well as 100 acres in "Diggs his Hundred." At this time he was listed as "Samuel Jordan of Charles Hundred gentleman."

Jordan himself died in 1623 and his widow was soon seeking marriage again. When she became betrothed to two men at the same time, Capt. William Ferrar and Rev. Greville Pooley, and became embroiled in controversy, the Council took note of it. A proclamation followed which prohibited any woman from contracting herself to "two several men at the same time."

Jordan's Journey seems to have prospered. In 1624 Nathaniel Causey represented the plantation in the Assembly. At the time there were forty-two persons in residence and eight had died within the year. In 1625 the population stood at fifty-five persons (thirty-six males and nineteen females). Corn and fish supplies were adequate and there were some cattle and hogs as well as numerous poultry. In the matter of houses, the total was quite large—being twenty-two. The plantation boasted of three boats and substantial amounts of small arms (thirty-eight) and armor of various types (thirty-six items).

WOODLEEFE'S PLANTATION (22)

Captain John Woodleefe, a member of the Virginia Company, came to Virginia initially in 1609 and remained active and interested in the Colony. He was commissioned, in 1619, to go as governor and commander of Berkeley Hundred which he did late in the year. He had other interests, however, and by April of the same year had brought four men, which he had supplied with "apparell and armes," and his wife and children to Virginia. It is intimated that he had other colonizing interests and intentions. The Berkeley Hundred people had cautioned him about attempting another plantation that might interfere with their holdings. He was instructed not to establish it "unless full ten English miles from them."

He was governor at Berkeley Hundred for about a year and it was sometime shortly before, during, or just after this term of service, that he set up his own plantation. He seems to have chosen a point on the south side of the James a bit up river from Berkeley which he patented in 1620. It lay along the river and west of Jordan's Journey. This could very well have been the 350 acres listed in his name in May, 1625. His was one of the tracts in "the territory of greate Weyanoke" and was later patented again by his son.

CHAPLAIN'S CHOICE (23)

This plantation appears in a listing in 1624. In March of that year, too, Isaac Chaplain represented it in the Assembly. This was another of the number of particular, or private, plantations founded in Virginia in the 1619-24 period. It is generally assumed to have been located in the area to the east of Woodleefe's Plantation. It was noted in May, 1625 that Isaac

Chaplain had 200 acres which were "planted" in the "territory of great Weyonoke." He had as well, what may have been a personal stake, 50 other acres in the Corporation of Charles City.

In 1624 a total of twenty-four persons were living "At Chaplains choice" and a year later the head count stood at seventeen (thirteen males, four females) This 1625 figure, as did the other muster statistics, included the Truelove Company people and goods. This embraced two boats, but only two houses, forty-one barrels of corn and some small amounts of peas, meal and oatmeal plus three hogs and forty-eight fowl. There were reasonable amounts of small arms and armor and six pieces of ordnance. The latter, an unusually high figure for a private plantation, included one falconet and five "murderers." Some tobacco was being produced, for "John Trehern of Chaplins Choise" exported "one hogshead" in 1625. A lawsuit ensued when the ship captain sold it, although it had been consigned to Trehern's brother. As satisfaction he was to get "two hundred & thirty waight of tobacco in leafe & smothed together with one hogshead."

TRUELOVE'S PLANTATION (24)

On January 24, 1621, a share of land in Virginia was assigned "unto Rowland Truelove of London, Clothworker." Three months later he received a patent as a "new adventurer" and in November, this was defined to cover the transportation of 100 persons. In this venture he had "divers other patentees, adventurers" and associates.

He does not appear to have been discouraged by the massacre, for in August, 1622, the Truelove Company sent supplies for their plantation. The Company records relate that "mr Trulove and his associates intend to proceed in their plantation beinge no whitt discouraged with this late massacre of the English by the treacherous Indians. . . ." They had requested a Commission for the "shippe and voyadge" to Virginia of the "barke called the *Trulove* of London of about forty-six tunn."

A year later, in July, 1623, "Rowland Treawlove and Companie" pledged anew to supply their plantation with "victuall apparrell and other necessaries" to the extent of £400. Their patent had recently been renewed, or passed again under the seal. This was one of seventy-two that passed in June, 1623 giving good evidence of the private activity afoot for, and in, the Colony at this time. Soon a ship was dispatched with twenty-five new emigrants. In the cargo, too, were 100 "hogsheads" of supplies valued at £536, a substantial sum, for the plantation of the Truelove Society.

Despite this, all did not go well and the enterprise seems not to have flourished. In January, 1624, Nathaniel Causey was directed by the Court in Virginia to "take into his hands and safe custodie all such goods as belonge to the Company and Societie of Trueloves Plantatione." This had been requested by the Company overseer and Causey, after a "true inventory" was to report to the Governor and Council. In the muster of 1625 Truelove's Plantation appears to be associated with Chaplain's Choice.

"POWLE-BROOKE" OR MERCHANT'S HOPE (25)

Captain Nathaniel Powell, who came early to Virginia and served as Acting Governor when Argall left in 1619, settled a plantation on the south side of the James. It was located on Powell Creek at the head of which was the site of Weyanoke Indian Town. The date of his establishment appears to have been in 1619, or a little later, and his enterprise embraced some 600 acres. It was known as "Powle Brook" and was not until later to get the Merchant's Hope designation.

Matters went well until the Indian massacre which all but wiped out the settlement and led to its abandonment. Captain Powell and his wife were both slain along with ten others, three of them women. It is said that the Indians were not content with killing. They proceeded to "butcher-like hagle their bodies, and cut off his head. . . ."

Powell's brothers and sisters in England petitioned the Company to get an account of the estate. The Company in turn asked the Virginia Council to take special care of "this buissnes, both because it is of great consequence, as also for that Captain Nath: Powell was a man of extraordinary merritt, and the petitioners poore men. . . ." Thomas Powell of Suffolk, England, came into the property. He, a brother of Nathaniel, later disposed of it by sale.

MAYCOCK'S PLANTATION (26)

Samuel Maycock came to Virginia about 1618 and served as a Councilor under both Yeardley and Wyatt. He located a plantation upriver from Jamestown on the south side next above Flowerdieu Hundred sometime prior to April, 1619. It took its name, Maycock's Hundred or Plantation, from him, the original patentee, as was often the case in early Virginia. It would seem that he, like others, then undertook to bring in men and supplies. There is reference to Sara Maycock bringing over four servants in the *Abigail* in 1622 "uppon the accompt of Mr. Samuell Maycock." For this she got 200 acres of her choice.

Maycock's was another of the early beginnings that was snuffed out by the massacre. Four were killed on his "Divident" including himself. Another was Edward Lister who came to Plymouth in the *Mayflower* and had signed the "compact." Maycock was one of six Councilors who perished on March 22, 1622 at the hand of the Indians.

FLOWERDIEU HUNDRED—PIERCEY'S HUNDRED (27)

In 1618 Sir George Yeardley acquired 1,000 acres on the south side of the James River above Martin's Brandon and across from his Tanks Weyanoke holding. He proceeded to establish a plantation here which he named in honor of his wife who had been Temperance Flowerdieu. In 1619 it was well enough along to merit the representation in the Assembly which was performed

71

by John Jefferson and Ensign Edward Rossingham, the latter one of Yeardley's kinsmen. This, perhaps, suffered in the massacre less than many other settlements. Only six persons were killed here. Flowerdieu Hundred was one of the fewer than a dozen points that the Colony decided to hold after the onslaught.

Council minutes and other sources in the 1622-24 period show the plantation as one that was probably functioning well. There were cases revolving around the use of livestock, particularly cattle, and the cultivation of tobacco. At least one such case led Yeardley to examine witnesses at "Flowerdieu Hundreth." One reference to tobacco puts interesting light on its cultivation at this time. Yeardley's overseer, one Sergeant Fortescue, was charged with negligence in the care of the harvested tobacco:

> . . . hee did hange the tobacco soe thick uppon the lynes that the lynes brake and the tobacco fell to the ground, and before the said tobaco was at all dryed he made it upp into role and soe by his faulte it was not marchantable and that all the tobacco except six or seven hundred waight, was made upp wett and nott merchantable, The whole crop amounting to 9000 waight or thereabouts.

This seems to mean a yearly harvest of 9,000 pounds at Flowerdieu Hundred in 1624.

This was the year that Yeardley sold this plantation as well as his holding across the James at Weyanoke to Captain Abraham Piercey, one of the leading merchants in the Colony. In 1624, the year of the sale, a population of sixty-three (including eleven negroes) had been listed for Flowerdieu Hundred with another eighteen having died in the previous twelve months. In the census of 1625, Piercey's Hundred, as the place was now called, had fifty-seven including its seven negroes (four men, two women and one child). The enumeration included twelve houses, three stores, four tobacco houses, and two boats, all of which had been bought, or built, by Piercey. There was a windmill too, and this, the first in the Colony, had been erected by Yeardley, it is said, in 1621. It stood on Windmill, earlier known as Tobacco, Point.

Corn supplies were given at ninety-three barrels and fish at 1,600 pounds. Cattle was totaled at forty-four head and hogs at thirty-one. Supplies of powder and lead were ample for the thirty-four "fixed pieces" which were on hand. Besides, there were thirty-four swords and 20 complete suits of armor as well as some other types. Two pieces of ordnance were included and, perhaps, one of these is that described as on hand in the winter of 1622. This evidently was one of the most successful of the Virginia private plantations.

"Captaine Spilmans Divident" (28)

Sometime prior to 1622 Captain Spilman, perhaps, Thomas Spilman, brother of Henry Spilman, occupied a tract that lay between Flowerdieu Hundred and Martin's Brandon. It was Thomas who had come to Virginia in 1616 or 1617. The massacre uprooted the settlement here and two persons were slain by the Indians. "Captaine Spilman, a man warie enough heretofore & acquainted with their trecheries," was forced to locate elsewhere. Thomas appears to have chosen Elizabeth City where he planted fifty acres and in 1625 was established with his wife, a child "borne in Virginia," and four servants.

Ward's Plantation (29)

Captain John Ward arrived in Virginia on April 22, 1619 in the ship *Sampson* with some fifty emigrants to establish a private plantation. Samuel Argall later placed this as in 1618. He selected some 1,200 acres west of Martin's Brandon and adjoining a creek on the south side of the James which still bears his name. He appears to have been in association with Captain John Bargrave who, for some years, had been intimately associated in Virginia trade and colonization. Several members of the Bargrave family were with him. It was Captain John Bargrave who, in 1622, claimed the distinction of having undertaken to be "the first planter of a private colony in Virginia." This effort he dated as late 1617, or early 1618, and it seemingly came to nought unless his effort was continued in the Ward and John Martin enterprises.

Both Ward and Bargrave were among those granted patents in 1619 and were included in the eleven people "Who had undertaken to transport to Virginia great multitudes of people, with store of cattell." Soon after arrival in the Colony, Ward found himself on the New England coast fishing to aid Virginia's food supply. On his return in July, he made his contribution to the general store.

His plantation evidently took root for it was among those that sent representatives to the first Assembly at Jamestown in July and August, 1619. Ward and his Lieutenant, John Gibbs, attended and Ward, himself, served on the Assembly committee that examined the first and third books of the "Great Charter."

Initially his representation was challenged on the grounds that he had seated in Virginia without authority and without a commission. The Burgesses, however, recognized his support of the Colony and the fact that he had adventured his person. He was permitted to take his seat providing he agree to get a lawful commission. There was no further question when he assented to this. Perhaps he fulfilled his obligation when his old indenture was passed again under the seal on May 17, 1620 in the name of "Capt John Warde and his associates."

Ward continued his activities and in the fall of 1620 he was again trading on the Potomac—"the people there, are said, to have dealt falsely with him, so he took 800 bushels of corne per force." Such acts probably had a bearing on the massacre that came in 1622. The massacre may, as a matter of fact, have ended the Ward Plantation story as it did the story for a number of settlements in early Virginia. Probably the twelve persons killed at Lieutenant Gibbs "Dividend" had reference to Ward's Plantation. Mention of the plantation ceases after this date although seemingly Ward received a new grant, or a reaffirmation of his old one, in June, 1623.

MARTIN'S BRANDON (30)

This private plantation, as did its founder John Martin, had a tumultuous history from the time of its establishment. Martin, a member of the first Virginia Council in 1607, lived almost constantly in the Colony for a quarter of a century. He will always be remembered as the single dissenting voice to the projected abandonment of Virginia in June, 1610. He, as James P. C. Southall, has stated was "in many ways . . . a typical Englishman in the sense that he was jealous and tenacious of his own rights, stubborn and courageous in maintaining them."

When in England in 1616-17 he "was allowed in reward ten shares" of Company stock and on January 29, 1617, obtained a patent that contained privileges and exemptions such as were never before, or after, granted to a Virginian planter. It was stipulated that he could "hold and enjoy" his Virginia lands "in as large & ample manner and to all intents & purposes as any Lord of Mannor here in England." It included, too, provision for "free trafick in the Bay and Rivers" and the right to establish "convenient markets" on his lands. He entered into close business partnership with Captain John Bargrave, whom the Company, in March, 1617, granted fifteen shares of land in Virginia. Bargrave "relying upon the said patent of Martin" proceeded to furnish the *"Edwyn* of London with men and wares of good value fit for the said plantation, and sent the same with the said Captain Martin into Virginia." Martin left England in April, 1617 on the *Edwin,* "a barke of very good sayle" and reached Virginia in May just after Argall who had come as governor.

Bargrave had been hopeful of trading with Martin's Brandon and transporting more colonists, yet Argall, to support the Colony, compelled the *Edwin* to remain in Virginia for almost a year and to be used in the Colony and on the coast. It was March, 1618 before it could set sail for England. In the meanwhile, Company affairs had come under different management and Martin's patent was under fire.

When the Assembly was called in 1619, his plantation, now being well established, sent two representatives down to Jamestown. The Burgesses challenged them saying that Martin's patent exempted his settlement from obedience to the laws of the Colony. Thomas Davis and Robert Stacy could be seated, it was ruled, if Martin would bring his patent into conformity. This he would not do saying that he would not "infringe any parte" of it. Thereupon, the General Assembly submitted the case to the Company for a definition and explanation of the offending clauses in Martin's patent. Later, exception was taken to the nature of the operation of Martin's Brandon plantation. It was alleged to be "a receptacle of vagabonds and bankrupts & other disorderly p[er]sons & whereof there hath been a public complaint. . . ." It was charged further to be a place "where such as are indebted do shroud and rescue them selves under his protection."

Martin proceeded to fight for his patent in England and did all that he could to maintain it. In the end, however, on April 2, 1623, he accepted a new one for the land to be "laid out in Martin's Brandon." He was denied the request for the nearby "swamps and boggs" for the use of "his swine."

When he had departed for England in the spring of 1621 he had left his settlement in the care of Lieutenant Edward Saunders. It was not until 1624 that Martin returned to Virginia with more servants and supplies. In the meanwhile the massacre had caused at least the temporary abandonment of the plantation after seven persons had been slain here. The area is not mentioned as such in either the population listing of 1624 or in the census of 1625. In the listing of land patents in 1625, however, there is an entry that reads "Marttin Brandon belonging to Captaine John Marttin by Patent out of England (planted)." A later deed

(1643) defines "Martin's Brandon" as 4,550 acres between Chippokes and Ward's Creeks.

"Paces-Paines" (31)

Richard Pace, late in 1620, braved the wilds over the river from Jamestown when, on December 5, he received a grant for 200 acres upstream from Jamestown. These acres became known as "the plantation called Paces Paines." It was in the territory of Tappahanna in the western extremity of the Corporation of James City. Adjoining him was the 100 acre tract granted, at the same time, to Francis Chapman who was described as "scituate nere unto Paces-Paines." This, a little later, was added to the Pace holdings. Pace was an "ancient planter" as was his wife Isabella who also took land in her own right. Their son George seated here and later claimed fifty acres each for the transportation of 6 persons in the *Marmaduke* in 1621. John Burrows became one of their neighbors.

Paces-Paines was seated soon after the patent was issued in 1620 and Richard, who produced tobacco here, reported later that he "bestowed great cost & charges uppon building ther, & cleareing of ground." He made this statement when he applied, successfully, for permission to return to his plantation some months after the massacre of 1622.

Both Pace and his plantation are mentioned in the accounts of this Indian uprising. As reported later, "if God had not put it into the heart of an Indian . . . to disclose it, the slaughter of the massacre could have been even worse." This Indian, one Chanco by name, belonged to William Perry. Perry was active in the Paces-Paines area and later married Richard Pace's widow and became "Commander" of the settlement. The night before the Indian attack Chanco was at Pace's. In the night he told Pace, who, it is reported, "used him as a sonne," of the impending danger. Whereupon Pace secured his own house and quickly crossed the river to Jamestown. The governor then spread the word as rapidly as possible undoubtedly saving many lives in the Jamestown area. Chanco, the Christian convert, has become a Virginia hero.

The retrenchment following the massacre led to the temporary abandonment of Paces-Paines; yet late in 1622 Pace returned, having promised to "fortifie & strengthen the place with a good company of able men." Although not listed in 1624, the settlement was among those enumerated in 1625. At that time it had a population of thirteen persons. It is of note, perhaps, that the census made no mention of Pace, or Perry, yet it does mention Francis Chapman as in residence. It included four old planters: John Proctor (1607), Phettiplace Close (1608), Thomas Gates (1609) and Francis Chapman (1608).

Burrows' Mount (32)

This, like Paces-Paines, was located on the south side of the James, upriver from Jamestown, and in the western part of the Corporation of James City. At the time of the census, early in 1625, it boasted of but seven persons. This, perhaps, should be increased by another ten suggested by the reference that "Mr. [John] Burrowes and six of his men which are planted heare are reconned, with theire armes provisions, etc. at *James Cittie*." His Jamestown listing actually included his wife, seven servants, and Mara Buck. He had become guardian for this daughter of the Rev. Richard Buck and this included the management of "the cattell belonging to Mr. Buck's children."

Burrows' Mount, or Burrows' Hill, was, it seems, a relatively new plantation early in 1625. Burrows' 150 acres here very likely were the result of his request for this amount on February 6 of that year. At that time the court awarded him, on presentation of the required "Certificates," the usual allotment for the transportation of three persons. His actual settlement at "Burrowes Mount" may, however, have preceded his grant.

78

Plantations "Over the river from Jamestown" (33)

Early in 1609 "We built also a fort for a retreat, near a convenient river, upon a high commanding hill, very hard to be assaulted, and easie to be defended: but ere it was halfe finished, this defect caused a stay," it is recorded in *The Proceedings of the English Colonies in Virginia* (1612). This was envisioned as a place of refuge in the event that enemy attack would force an evacuation of Jamestown. It is now assumed that this was about a mile up a creek directly across the river from Jamestown and that it still exists in part.

The fort saw no service. As a matter of fact, the colonists evidently did not, in the first decade, find the south shore of the James across from "James Citty" particularly hospitable. There is little record of activity here prior to the massacre in March, 1622, although some land grants may have preceded it.

Captain William Powell traded acres here with Captain John Hurleston as early as 1620. A court case in 1625 establishes that Captain Powell and others "did cleere a piece of grounde" here in April, 1622 which later fell to Captain Samuel Mathews. This embraced some eight or nine acres and did involve "howses" as well. On April 23, 1623, there was reference to "all the plantations right over against James Citty." They were described as pleasant and fruitful seats. The area in question here extended from Hog Island up to the projection of land now called Swan's Point.

The plantations were represented as a group in the Assembly of 1624 by Samuel Mathews and Edward Grindon. Collectively, in 1624, they had a reported population of thirty-three. In that year twenty-one persons died, two having been slain by the Indians. It is not until the census of 1625 that a number of the plantations in this section are clearly identified. Five such are listed with a total population of ninety-six persons. This was clearly a growing community at this time.

In May, 1625, it is of record that in excess of 3,700 acres had been taken up in "The territory of Tappahanna over against James Citie" by sixteen persons. Eleven of the grants were noted as "planted." The largest single grant was to William Ewens for 1,000 acres. It should be noted, perhaps, that no acreage figure was shown for the "Divident" of Captain Samuel Mathews and that of Captain John Hurleston. Among those listed as having received grants, and some were dead, were John Rolfe (400 acres), Richard Pace (200 acres), Captain William Powell (750 acres in two parcels), George Sandys (300 acres), and John Burrows (150 acres). All were "planted." Only the acreage of John Dodd, Francis Chapman, Thomas Gates, John Utie and Robert Evers were not "planted."

THE TREASURER'S PLANTATION (GEORGE SANDYS) (33A)

George Sandys was named resident treasurer of the Colony and came to Virginia in the ship *George* in 1621. He, it seems, soon became interested in the area over the water from Jamestown. His patent for 300 acres, here, as Treasurer of Virginia, is dated in December, 1624, yet he was already "actually possessed" of this dividend, 100 acres of which was for a bill of adventure for a share of Company stock and 200 for the transportation of four persons to Virginia in 1621. He had William Claiborne survey "at his plantation over the water" 650 acres including his and parcels belonging to John Bainham and Edward Grindon. This was "by the water side" and was about a square mile in extent as reported by Claiborne. Evidently Sandys was actually in possession of all three tracts at the time of the survey.

In 1625 his plantation had seventeen servants including two boys, and Daniel Poole, "a french man" with his wife and "a yong child of theires." Poole was defined as a "hired" man. Besides his own people, another twenty-two lived "in the Treasurors Plant." In this number were two women and several Italians.

80

His was, perhaps, one of the best equipped plantations in Virginia. There were two dwellings, cabins, two stores, a framed house for raising silkworms, a vineyard of two acres, and an acre and a half garden as well as "one large fort palled in" and a piece of mounted ordnance. His 100 barrels of corn was the largest amount reported by any single plantation. His arms were extensive—thirty "armours" of various types, thirty small arms and twenty swords. He was, however, a little short on livestock having only nine goats and kids and two hogs.

HUGH CROWDER'S PLANTATION (33B)

Crowder came to Virginia in 1619 and became interested in a group ground clearing project across the water as early as April, 1622. He reported that "six of his family did help to cleere that grounde." In this he was joined by Captain William Powell, Richard Pace, William Perry, Richard Richards and Thomas Garses.

In 1625 Crowder was living on land here that earlier had been claimed by Captain John Hurleston who exchanged it about Christmas time in 1620 with Captain William Powell. At the time of the census of 1625 Crowder's Plantation evidently was a small one. He was in residence along with five male servants, one a boy of fourteen years of age.

EDWARD BLANEY'S PLANTATION (33C)

Blaney's muster of 1625 included fifteen men all in the age group from seventeen to forty with most being under thirty. He, it seems, was not in residence here over the water. In 1624 he had represented Jamestown in the Assembly and was still living in "James Citty" in 1625. He was a prominent man of affairs and was one of the thirty-one signers of the planters' answer to the attack on the administration of Colony affairs during its first twelve years.

Capt. Roger Smith's Plantation (33D)

Smith came to Virginia in 1620 and a year later was named to the Council, being first designated a "provisionall Councellor" on July 12, 1621. He, it might be added, married Jane, the widow of John Rolfe who is thought to have been killed in 1622. Perhaps, this gave him use of the land across the James which Rolfe is reported to have patented.

In 1625 Captain Smith seemingly was, like Edward Blaney, in residence at "James Citty." He had at his plantation over the river, however, a small group of nine men one of whom had his wife with him. These were well armed as were most of those living in this area at the time.

Capt. Samuel Mathews' Plantation (33E)

Samuel Mathews, long time a councilor in Virginia beginning in 1624, first came to Virginia, it appears, in 1620. In November, 1622 there is reference to a patent granted to him for undertaking to transport 100 persons to the Colony. About a month later he seems to have been interested in Captain Powell's cleared ground across the water from Jamestown. Mathews evidently seated on it and Powell loaned him "the howses of the upper fort for the use of his servants." In 1625 the court saw no way to "put Captain Samuell Mathews who is presently seated thereon, out of possessione" in spite of a petition to do this.

In a listing of land grants in 1625, there is reference to Mathews "Divident planted" although no acreage is mentioned. The same list indicated that Powell had earlier received two tracts of 200 and 550 acres respectively, both of which were now "planted" over the water from Jamestown.

At the time of the census in 1625 Mathews' plantation had a single muster. It consisted of a minister, Rev. David Sands, himself and twenty-three men who were all listed as servants. The plantation apparently had no women in it. The scarcity of

82

wives and children in this, as in most of the plantations here, would indicate a lack of settled conditions. Perhaps this was to be expected in an area which had not long been opened to actual settlement as seems to have been generally true of this section.

Hog Island (34)

This low marshy area on the south side of the river at the wide bend of the James some five miles below Jamestown appears in the records as early as January, 1609. At that time Mathew Scrivener, a Councilor, and nine others "would needs visit the Ile of hogges." A mishap occurred and the entire party was drowned en route. Perhaps this was just before "the hogges [at Jamestown] were transported to Hog Ile, where also we built [in 1609] a blocke house with a garrison, to give us notice of any shipping; and for their exercise, they made clapboard, wainscott, and cutt downe trees against the ships comming." Evidently when the three sows in one year increased to 60 and odd "piggs" it proved too much for the fort and its environs at Jamestown. In 1610 there was another reference to the "Ile of Hogs" and then all is silence for a decade. The doubtful safety of the spot, its inconvenience, and its distance from Jamestown probably caused its abandonment as a suitable place for quartering the Colony's supply of hogs.

In 1619 a request for a grant of 300 acres of marsh land in the area called "Hogg Iland" was made to the Company, yet precise assignment was not approved since the Court in England correctly stated that it did not know "who allredie may lay clayme thereunto or otherwise how necessary itt may be for the publique." On March 28, 1619, Governor Argall proclaimed "Hog Island" within the bounds of Jamestown and granted "inhabitants of Jamestown" the right to plant here as in other parts of the area as "members of the corporation and parish of the same." There is still, however, no record of a settlement here and no references to losses in the massacre.

A year later the picture evidently had changed. In February, 1623, there is mention of "Ensigne John Utie at Hog-Ileand" in instructions involving the shipment of "three score thousand waight of sasafras" to be raised on a levy basis in Virginia. In November, 1624, this John Utie received a grant of 100 acres at Hog Island for the transportation, in 1623, of two persons to Virginia. He, it seems, was here before his patent came through. The settlement apparently grew rapidly as the 1624 population listing enumerates thirty-one persons for Hog Island and the census of 1625 shows fifty-three persons. Although not represented in the Assembly of 1619, it had two representatives, Burgesses, in the Assembly of 1624, John Utie and John Chew. Chew, who came to Virginia in 1620 and became a prominent merchant, also had property at Jamestown.

Still another prominent figure at Hog Island was Ralph Hamor. In May, 1624, he filed suit in the general court against Robert Evers. It would appear that John Bailey received a grant from Governor Yeardley about 1617 for 490 acres on Hog Island. He did not seek to improve his land and seemed reluctant to locate it specifically. Hamor, too, had a "particular patent" from the Company in England "which patent was burnt in the massacre." Moreover he had "a purpose to settle a plantacion already begunne upon an island, called Hog Island." Reference would indicate that other areas, too, had been "cleared & seated upon" including one "parcell of land cleered by Southampton Hundred Company." The end result was that Robert Evers, guardian for Mary, John Bailey's daughter, should see to it that the original grant be selected and "survayde and laid owte in hogg Islande." Any "surplusage" would go to the next claimant in line, but Captain Hamor would have to be satisfied "for the buildinge of such howses & cleringe of land as he shall build and cleare, till the right be decided." Hamor, who already had his dwelling house here, seemingy obtained some 250 acres in the end.

The 1625 muster would indicate that Hamor was not in residence although he had seven servants here. It shows, too, that Sir George Yeardley was in the picture with fifteen men at Hog Island, three listed as "Dwellers." Five houses were listed but only nine hogs, a number too small to be impressive. There was some armor, a good supply of small arms and, comparatively speaking, an adequate stock of corn of 30 barrels. All of this speaks of an established settlement.

LAWNE'S PLANTATION (35)

It was in the spring of 1619 that Capt. Christopher Lawne's "private plantation" was established. A ship bearing some 100 emigrants and supplies, sent out by Richard Wiseman, Nathaniel Basse and others reached Virginia and located on the south side of the James River below Hog Island. Among other things he was to have provided twenty men for the common Company land; however, he reduced this to fifteen when the expected "loane of corne and cattle" was not forthcoming.

He and his men apparently, as was reported later, proceeded effectively to plant the land he had been granted "accordinge to the purpose of theire patentes." This was one of four private patents issued in the first twelve years of the Virginia settlement, the others being that of Samuel Argall, Martin's Hundred, and John Martin. The Company, on November 5, 1618, had acted to encourage these particular Hundreds and it had been specified that they could return what commodities they could produce to their own adventurers. They could buy from goods in the general store, if available; however, they could not trade for other commodities produced in Virginia.

In July, 1619, Lawne's settlement was noted to be a new plantation recently seated. It was, however, eligible for representation in the Assembly and Lawne and Ensign Washer journeyed up to Jamestown to attend the Assembly meeting that summer. In November, 1619, when "the danger of his seate beinge far from any other Englishe Plantacon in the bottom of the bay of Warrestoyack" was mentioned Lawne expressed confidence that he could "make the place good against the Indians beinge a necke land and defended by his howse. . . ." Besides, he expected in emergency to team up with "Lieftennant Basse and Ensigne Washer." Together they could muster "a party of thirtye men."

Shortly, Lawne became ill and because of "his owne sicknes and his peoples, wherein there was improvidency" he quit his plantation and went up to Charles City where he died. One contemporary commented that "so his project is likely, unles better followed and well seconded, to come to nothing." More was to come. Nathaniel Basse, John Hobson, Richard Wiseman and other fellow adventurers, with Captain Christopher Lawne deceased, "applied for and received, on November 13, 1620," a "confirmacon of their old pattent" in which it was specified that henceforth it would be called the "Ile of Wightes Plantacon." The heirs of Lawne were to be protected and the Company allowed five years to bring the settlement up to strength. A little later Nathaniel Basse went on to establish a plantation known for a time as "Basse's Choyce."

WARRASCOYACK (BENNETT'S PLANTATION) (36)

Located on the south side of the James River above Nansemond, this plantation took its name from the Indians of the locality. It, along with several other sites which included Martin's Hundred, and Pasbehegh, was described as a "verie fruitful and pleasant" seat, "free from salt mariches beinge all on the fresh river and . . . [a] verie healthfull and high land." This was unlike "James Citty" even though Jamestown was "as high as Debtforde or Ratcliffe." Warrascoyack was known, too, as Bennett's Plantation, and as "Bennetes Wellcome" after Edward Bennett, a well established London merchant, who, with others of his family, established it as a "particular" plantation.

Bennett, who was admitted to the Virginia Company on

April 12, 1621, obtained a patent the next October. At the time it was noted that he "had deserved singularly well of the Company before he was a member thereof, and since his admittance hee had been att a verie great charge for transportinge of people to Virginia. . . ." On November 21, 1621, he was issued a patent for 100 "planters." This undoubtedly explains how quickly Warrascoyack was settled.

It was evidently well established in the spring of 1622 when there is reference to the "houses wherein Warresquiocke people were placed." This, it should be added, was not the only plantation to be contemplated in the Warrascoyack district. Captain Christopher Lawne, in 1619, for example, was in the general area having been located just to the north of where Bennett's patent was fixed and "Basses Choyse" was not far away to the south, downstream.

The Indian massacre was disastrous to the Warrascoyack settlement. More than 50 men and women were slain *"at* Mr. Edward Bennett's Plantation" including the commander "Master Th: Brewood, his wife, his childe, two servants." Perhaps, the Indians remembered the fall of 1610 when Edward Brewster and Samuel Argall fell upon their Chief and burned two of his townes accusing him of "acting falsely." There had been no hint of destruction when the Indians returned "one Browne" two days before the onslaught. Browne had been living with them to learn their language.

Following the massacre Governor Wyatt ordered Captain Ralph Hamor to "bring away all the people and goodes from Wariscoyack upp to James Cittie" for safety. The military expedition against the natives may not have been wholly successful or perhaps, there were other reasons that delayed the return to Warrascoyack. Such might be inferred from Bennett's request to the Company on October 7, 1622 "that his people might be returned to his plantacon at Warascoacke." He was given leave for the "repossessinge."

In April, 1623, the Governor by proclamation ordered the building of a fort at Warrascoyack. This, "to defend . . . against the invasion of any forreine ennimy," was more against external than internal foes. It was to be by public subscription and to be carried out under Captain Roger Smith's direction in six months. It was known to require "great ordnance." Two years later, however, it had not been effected although it was still considered a good point from which "to secure the places above."

Evidently the massacre produced but a temporary delay at Warrascoyack. The picture painted in a letter from Richard to Edward Bennett on June 9, 1623, written from Bennett's Welcome, was one of new supplies, fears of encroachments, growth and thankfulness: "Our men stande well to ther helthe God be thanced and I hope to make you a good crope, bothe for tobaco and corne. The forte is abuildinge apase." The Indians were still respected nonetheless and the plan called for an expedition "to cute downe their corne and put them to sorde" after "we have wedid our Tobaco and cornne." It was a little later in the year that William Bennett, the minister at Warrascoyack, sued for his two years of back salary—1,533 ⅓ pounds of tobacco.

In 1624 the plantation was represented in the Assembly by one John Pollington. In fact, in that year, the settlement had thirty-three persons including three negroes even though twenty-six had died in the preceding twelve months period. A year later, in 1625, the population had dropped to nineteen. A dozen more deaths were recorded including five "slayne by the Indianes." Mortality continued high at Warrascoyack ("Warwick Squeake" as it was occasionally designated).

In the February, 1625 census listings, there were two houses, a store, and two palisadoes. Armament was light, consisting of nine suits of armor and thirteen "fixed pieces." The largest of the four musters was that which listed the twelve servants of Edward Bennett. The others were one, two, and four persons respectively. Before May, 1625 it was reported out of Virginia that some 1,750 acres of land had been patented at "Warras-quoake plantacon downe wards from Hogg Island xiiii miles, by the river side." This included 300 acres "planted" by Captain Nathaniel Basse.

"BASSE'S CHOYSE" (37)

In November, 1621, the Virginia Company voted a patent to Arthur Swayne and Nathaniel Basse, adventurers, and to their associates to transport 100 persons to Virginia. This patent for a "particular plantation" was further confirmed in January, 1622. Basse evidently proceeded to execute the necessary measures to translate this into reality. He was in Virginia in October, 1622.

Basse located in the Warrascoyack area downstream from Bennett's Plantation and proceeded to establish his settlement. In 1624 he represented it in the Assembly. About this time the settlement numbered some twenty persons, but a year later it had only twelve in four separate musters. The even dozen inhabitants included three women and a child, "borne in Virginia," all indicating family life rather than a military outpost. Arms and weapons were in plentiful supply nonetheless: twenty-two "armours" of various types, twenty small arms, four pistols, twelve swords and two pieces of ordnance. There was ample corn, a good fish supply and seven houses to give the settlement comfort.

Basse, it appears, had planted by patent some 300 acres and his neighbor to the north was interested in his activity. In June, 1623 Robert Bennett wrote to Edward Bennett in Virginia asking that he report whether Basse, or others, might "claim anye lande as ther righte" in the Bennett's Welcome sphere.

NANSEMOND (38)

A settlement was attempted on an island in the Nansemond River in the late summer of 1609, yet it was of short duration. With Jamestown overpopulated, due to the arrival of the third supply, and dissension rife, Smith sent out several parties with supplies to establish other posts. For the Nansemond effort, he dispatched sixty men under the command of Captain John Martin and George Percy. The expedition moved partly by water and partly by land and consolidated in the Nansemond River. When efforts "to barter with . . . [the Indian Chief] for an island righte opposite ageinste the maine . . . [for] copper hatches and other comodeties" failed, the island was seized by force with little concern for the natives who proved wholly unhospitable. "So haveinge scene Capte: Martin well settled I [George Percy] retourned with Capte Nellson to James Towne ageine acordinge to apoyntementts."

The Indians continually attacked the settlement and the good supplies of corn in the area could not be utilized. For reasons of business and safety Martin journeyed up to Jamestown. Reinforcements helped not at all. A party sent from Nansemond to trade at Kecoughtan was not heard from and many of the settlers were killed in skirmishes in the area of the island post. In late fall, it was necessary for all survivors to return to Jamestown, as Percy relates, "to feede upon the poore store we had lefte us."

THE EASTERN SHORE (39)

The census of early 1625 showed clearly that the colonization of the area across the Chesapeake Bay was secure. The enumeration listed a total of fifty-one persons, a decline from the seventy-six persons named the year before. The listing of property and accommodations, however, showed stability and establishment. This embraced twenty dwellings and seventeen stores, the latter, perhaps, suggesting an active Indian trade which had long been a hopeful prospect here. There was, too, a fort and a substantial listing of arms: thirty-five firearms, three swords and twenty-eight armors as well as 155 pounds of powder and 646 pounds of shot. The inhabitants were classified as thirty-two free, seventeen servants and two children (forty-four males, seven females). The Company's and Secretary's tenants were seated on their respective lands although they had not yet been surveyed. The several distinct musters included those of Charles Harman, John Blore, and Captain John Willcockes as well as "Ancient" Thomas Savage. The largest was that of Captain William Epes who could count thirteen servants. All were grouped on the Bay side of the lower part of the peninsula and, although not contiguous, formed a compact group in "The Kingdome of Acchawmacke."

This was in a sense the most isolated of all Virginia plantations being separated from the main body of the settlement by the wide waters of the Chesapeake. It enjoyed, however, a healthful climate, fruitful land and waters, and a continuing friendly Indian population.

As early as June, 1608, an exploring group under John Smith had made a landing on the Eastern Shore and visited the Indian "King of Accawmacke." They learned much of the area including the observation that the natives fished "with long poles like javelings, headed with bone." This was the beginning of a lasting friendship with "Laughing King," a friendship which was strengthened by Thomas Savage, the young boy exchanged with Powhatan in 1608, who later went to dwell across the Bay.

In 1613 Samuel Argall, seeking fish for the James River settlements as well as trade, visited the Eastern Shore. He found people "who seemed very desirous of our love." He traded successfully for corn, found great store of fish and then explored along the outer islands observing that "salt might easily be made there, if there were any ponds digged, for that I found salt kerned where the water had overflowne in certain places."

Argall's thoughts about salt manufacture were followed up in June, 1614 when a group of some twenty men under Lieutenant Craddock was dispatched to the area to set up a salt works and to catch fish. This was the first settlement "across the Bay" and it was known as "Dale's Gift" after Sir Thomas Dale then deputy governor in Virginia. The site selected for the work was on Smith's Island along the outer edge of the point of the peninsula.

The quarters for the workmen may have been built on the mainland just above the point of the peninsula long known as Cape Charles.

Dale's Gift endured for a time although it appears to have been abandoned during Argall's administration. It was one of only six points of settlement as listed for Virginia in 1616. John Rolfe's description of it at this time shows its garrison-like quality: "At Dales Gifte (lieng upon the sea neere unto Cape Charles, about thirty miles from Kequoughtan) are seventeen [men] under the command of one Leiftenaunte Cradock; all these are fed and maintained by the Colony. Their labor is to make salte; and to catch fishe at the two seasons aforemencioned [spring and fall]." The work was allowed to lapse and in 1620 the "salt works" were described as "wholly gone to rack and let fall" with serious consequences. It led, it appears, to some "distemper" in Virginia caused by the colonists "eating pork and other meats fresh and unseasoned." In any case measures were taken in 1620-21 to re-establish the works and Pory reported that he had found a suitable spot not far from "where was our salt-house."

Permanent colonization of the Eastern Shore dates, it seems, from about 1619 when Thomas Savage went there to live on a large tract of land lying between Cheriton and King's Creek (Savage's Neck) given him by "Laughing King" (Debedeavon). Savage, as reported by John Martin who visited there in April, 1619, was already well established in Indian councils. Both Savage and Martin recognized the value of trade with the Indians here as did John Pory who visited the Eastern Shore in 1621. Pory, Secretary of the Colony, had been authorized the year before to lay out 500 acres and to place 20 men on them for the support of his office. This he did sending 10 men in 1620 and 10 more in 1621. In 1621, too, John Willcox planted across the bay. In this same year Sir George Yeardley obtained a large acreage from Debedeavon. When Yeardley, in June, 1622, crossed the bay to inspect his property he was so pleased with what he saw that he stayed six weeks. There had been no massacre here for "Laughing King" had refused to join in the Indian plot. He had, in fact, warned the Governor of the impending catastrophe. The area across the Bay had also escaped the "foull distemper" that swept along the James plantations about this time. Mortality had been high from the epidemic that probably came from the newly arriving immigrants to Virginia.

The Eastern Shore was now well established. In 1624 its first representatives, Captain John Willcox and Henry Watkins, were sent to the Assembly which met at Jamestown in March. It appears that a minister, the Rev. Francis Bolton, served here for a time. Others moved over from the western shore including Lady Elizabeth, widow of Sir Thomas Dale. Few, it seems, came directly from Europe to Virginia's Eastern Shore. Most came after a sojourn in one, or more, of the settlements along the James.

ELIZABETH CITY (KECOUGHTAN) (40)

Early in 1625 the community of Elizabeth City, or rather the communities that made up Elizabeth City, could count some 359 persons. This included those "Beyond Hampton River" earlier referred to as "At Bucke Row." In the year before, 1624, this area had counted some 349 (thirty at "Bucke Roe") and in that year a total of 101 had died. These figures indicate both a high mortality as well as a high rate of immigration into this section. Elizabeth City, in 1625, was the largest community in Virginia, much larger than James City and its Island with its 175 persons (218 in 1624), which held second place in population.

In 1625 it was an established community including 279 males and eighty females. Four were negroes. More than twenty-five per cent were living beyond Hampton River. It had the large total of eighty-nine houses besides twenty stores, all beyond Hampton River, and twenty-four palisadoes. Its supplies of corn and fish were large and ample compared with other settlements although it was weak in livestock and poultry when viewed in comparison with Jamestown and some of the upriver communities. Although strong in small arms, it had a major allotment of ordnance. It did boast of six boats. Excepting Jamestown, this was the largest fleet in the Colony although the Eastern Shore was close with its five.

There were fifty-four separate musters or groups in Elizabeth City with the largest of them being that of Capt. William Tucker including his wife and daughter, "borne in Virginia in August," and eighteen others. Among these were three negroes, Antoney, Isabell and "William theire Child Baptised." There was, too, the muster of the ancient planters John and Anne Laydon and their four girls, all Virginia "borne." The oldest of them was the first child born in the Colony. Nicolas Martiau was listed here, as was Ensign Thomas Willoby and Edward Waters. In addition to the fifty-four musters, or groups, in Elizabeth City proper there were sixteen resident beyond Hampton River. These embraced Captain Francis West and Sergeant William Barry. The latter had fifteen servants which was a larger number than most musters enumerated. It appears that in excess of 4,000 acres of land had been patented and the greater part of it had been planted. Patents, too, had been issued for land across the Hampton Roads on the south side of the James River, yet none is listed as having been planted at this date.

Elizabeth City began on the site of an Indian village on the west side of Hampton Creek and was known by its Indian name of Kecoughtan for a decade. The English first saw this spot on May 1, 1607 when the three ships moved over from Cape Henry. The friendly Indians welcomed the shore party and took them to their village of some 18 houses of twigs and bark and twenty fighting men where there was food, a friendly smoke, and entertainment.

After this visit the settlers moved on up the James and it was fall before the English were here again. John Smith then traded successfully with them for corn. Smith was here again in the summer of 1608 and in the following winter always being well received and refreshed before leaving. There is clear evidence that the first post established by the Colonists for trade with the Indians was here where Indians and whites lived together in some number. When, however, Humphry Blunt out of Fort Algernourne, that is Old Point Comfort, was killed by Indians at Nansemond, Sir Thomas Gates used the opportunity to punish the Indians by driving the Kecoughtans away from their cornfields and fishing grounds. It was in the summer of 1610 that he "posseseinge himselfe of the Towne and the fertill ground there unto adjacentt haveinge well ordered all things he lefte his Lieftenantt Earley to comawnd his company and retourned to James Towne."

In October, 1609, after Smith's departure for England, President George Percy had sent Captain John Ratcliffe down to the mouth of the river to erect a fort due to "the plenty of the place for fisheinge" and "for the comodious discovery of any shippeinge which sholde come uppon the co[a]ste." He chose Point Comfort, so named in 1607, and designated it "Algernowns Foarte" after Lord De La Warr's "name and howse." When Ratcliffe was killed by the Indians while on an expedition up the York, Captain James Davis was named to command in his stead.

Those at Point Comfort in the winter of 1609-10 apparently fared much better than those at Jamestown. When Percy visited here he found them, he reports, "in good case and well lykeinge haveinge concealed their plenty from us above att James Towne beinge so well stored thatt the crabb fishes where with they fede their hoggs wold have bene a greate relefe unto us and saved many of our lykes."

It was on the Kecoughtan site that an English settlement (Hampton) began to evolve. For two or three years it was little more than a military outpost and a plantation where corn was grown to help fill the larder at Jamestown. To supplement the fort at Point Comfort, De La Warr had two more built on either side of a small stream, Fort Henry and Fort Charles. This river De La Warr called the Southampton (Hampton), the name that came to be applied, too, to the wide waters into which it flowed, Hampton Roads. The forts were intended both as strongholds against the Indians and as a rest stop, or acclimation point, for incoming settlers "that the weariness of the sea may be refreshed in this pleasing part of the countree."

The forts were abandoned in the fall, but when Sir Thomas Dale reached Point Comfort on May 22, 1611, he reoccupied them. He left James Davis in command of Fort Algernourne and proceeded to restore Fort Charles on the east side of, and Fort Henry on the west side of, Hampton River before going on to Jamestown.

It was in 1611 that a Spanish caravel appeared at Point Comfort, picked up an English pilot and sailed away leaving three of its crew. One of them was the spy Diego de Molina who later reported that Fort Algernourne had a garrison of twenty-five and four iron pieces. A fire destroyed the fort, except for Captain Davis' house and storehouse. He, however, rebuilt it with "expedition." In 1614 "Point Comfort Fort" as Fort Algernourne was called after Percy left in April, 1612, was described as a stockade "without brick or stone" containing fifty persons (men, women and boys), protected by seven iron pieces. Soon after this the fort evidently fell into disuse.

In 1613 each of the forts on Hampton River had fifteen soldiers but no ordnance and in 1614 Capt. George Webb was the principal commander of both. Ralph Hamor at this time described them as "goodly seats and much corne ground about them, abounding with the commodities of fish, fowle, deere and fruits, whereby the men live there, with halfe that maintenaunce out of the store, which in other places was allowed." He thought it an excellent spot except "we cannot secure it, if a forraigne enemy, as we have just caus to expect daily should attempt it."

The settlement grew slowly as the report of John Rolfe in 1616 shows: "At Keqoughtan, being not farr from the mouth of the river, thirty-seven miles below James Towne on the same side, are twenty [persons] whereof eleven are Farmors. All these also mayntayne themselves as the former. Captain George Webb Commander, Mr. William Mays Mynister there."

At this time it ranked fifth in size of the then existing six Virginia settlements. Only Dale's Gift on Eastern Shore was smaller. The largest at the time was Bermuda Hundred with its 119 persons. Jamestown was second with fifty. Although small it can be assumed that since 1611, although much a military post, it was changing. Rolfe relates that there were women and children "in every place some" and where there are women and children there is family life.

In 1619 the settlement of Kecoughtan was captained by William Tucker and he and William Capps represented the settlement in the first House of Burgesses. It was evidently on their petition that the Assembly was asked "to change the savage name of Kiccowtan, and to give that Incorporation a new name." It was so ordered, and the new name was Elizabeth City after the daughter of King James.

The next five years saw extensive growth in this area including the assignment of 3,000 acres of Company land, 1,500 acres for common use and 100 acres for a glebe. In 1620 some Frenchmen were sent to the Buck Roe section to instruct the colonists in planting mulberries and vines and in sericulture and viniculture. In 1621 Captain Thomas Newce came as manager of the Company lands and obtained a grant of 600 acres for himself. The resident minister at the time was Reverend James Stockton who took a rather dim view of Indian character.

The massacre of 1622 did not leave any dead at Elizabeth City. This appears to have been due in part to the good work of Captain Newce who took defensive measures and made plans to alleviate the suffering resulting from the Indian devastation. The massacre stimulated the growth of population in Elizabeth City which still, however, was not immune from Indian attack as witnessed by the four who were killed in September, 1622.

William Tucker of Elizabeth City was one of those whom Wyatt called on to lead punitive attacks on the Indians. Following these the Indian threat to Elizabeth City was essentially removed and the area came to enjoy peace and freedom for development as was reflected in the census of 1624 and that of 1625. In 1623 it was called in one document "the first plantation." The· Elizabeth City community embraced the sites of Point Comfort, Fort Charles, Fort Henry, and Kecoughtan, west of Hampton Creek, as well as the areas of Buck Roe, "Strawberry Banks," east of Hampton Creek, and "Indian Thickett."

Newport News (41)

The English first saw the site of Newport News on May 2, 1607 as they ascended the James River en route to Jamestown. There is, however, no reference to an Indian site here or to any specific use of the area, which Smith listed as "Point Hope" on his map of Virginia, until more than a decade later, November, 1621 when Daniel Gookin settled here. It is reported that "at Nupor[t]s-newes: the cotton trees in a yeere grew so thicke as ones arme, and so high as a man: here; any thing that is planted doth prosper so well as in no other place better."

A brief account penned by David Pietersz de Vries, a Dutch shipmaster, who visited Virginia in March, 1633 implies that Newport News then was an established watering point for incoming, and even outgoing, vessels. His description tends to provoke the thought that such had been the case for years, perhaps from the early days of Virginia. "The 10th, we sailed up the river [James]. When we came to the before-mentioned point of Newport-Snuw, we landed and took in water. A fine spring lies inside the shore of the river, convenient for taking water from. All the ships come here to take in water on their way home.

After we had procured some water, we sailed on. . . . ." On March 20, when leaving Virginia, De Vries observed again "anchored at evening before the point of Newport-Snuw, where we took in water."

The earliest known reference to the name Newport News is in a letter written from Jamestown on November 11, 1619 when the inhabitants of Kecoughtan were assured the opportunity "to choose ther divident alonge the banke of the great river betweene Kequohtan and Newportes Newes." The origin of its name is obscure yet it is not unlikely that Captain Christopher Newport is honored here. A second reference, one in January, 1620 lists "Newports Newes." Later references, in the Virginia Company records (1621-24), show varying forms: "Newportnewes," "Nuports Newes," "New ports-newes" and "Newport newes." The name seems established before Gookin and his friends, the Newces, entered the scene; hence it is improbable that Newce or Newcetown, Ireland, is responsible for the name. The name "Newportes Poynte" is shown on Robert Tindall's map of 1608 but it refers to a point on the York River rather than to the Newport News site.

Daniel Gookin was a friend and associate of Sir William Newce and Captain Thomas Newce, both prominent in Virginia affairs, yet not of long time in the Colony, and like them was from Newcetown in Ireland. All had plans to establish a strong settlement in Virginia. As early as November, 1620, the Company had agreed to pay Gookin to transport some livestock to Virginia. He was promised a patent in Virginia for a "particular" plantation. His arrival and establishment, late in 1621, is recorded in a letter of the governor and council in January, 1622:

There arived heere about the 22th of November a shipp from mr Gookine out of Ireland wholy uppon his owne adventure, withoute any relatione at all to his contract with you in England which was soe well furnished with all sortes of provisione, as well as with cattle, as wee could wishe all men would follow theire example, hee hath also brought with him aboute fifty more uppon the adventure besides some thirty other passengers, wee have accordinge to their desire seated them at Newportes news, and we doe conceave great hope (if the Irish plantacone prosper) that frome Ireland greate multitudes of people wilbe like to come hither . . . .

His plantation did, it seems, prosper, yet not without loss in men and effort. In the spring of 1623 when forty new men reported to the settlement things were not good. "Of all Mr. Gookins men which he sent out the last year we found but seven, the rest being all killed by the Indians, and his plantation ready to fall to decay." At the time of the Indian massacre he refused to take refuge in a stronger place deeming his settlement strong enough to withstand attack. With thirty-five men he succeeded in this and, it seems, was the first to reach England with news of the massacre. His son Daniel Gookin, Jr., evidently took over the management of the settlement when he left.

The census of 1625 from "Newportes newes" lists only the muster of Daniel Gookin and would indicate that neither he, nor his son, was in residence at the time. The listing shows only a total of twenty servants, eight of whom came in the *Flyinge Hart* in 1621 and twelve of the forty who had come in the *Providence* in 1623. The entire population was male and evidently they lived in four houses; at least only four were reported. At the time corn supplies stood at thirty barrels and cattle numbered fifteen head. For arms, the plantation had sixteen fixed pieces, twenty swords, and three pieces of ordnance. It would seem that the area of the plantation embraced 1,300 patented acres all of which were "planted."

In January, 1624 it had been sufficiently strong to be included in the Governor's instructions to Captain William Tucker, of Elizabeth City. These called for the meeting of "all the free men inhabiting in those plantacons under your comand at Keycotan & Nuport Newes [for the purpose of] by pluralitie of voices to make election of twoe men" to attend the General Assembly called for February. Of the four who were chosen from the "Incorporation of Elizabeth City," however, two were from Elizabeth City proper and two from "Elizabeth City beyond Hampton River." None was from Newport News.

BLUNT POINT (42)

The extent of settlement in this area on the north side of the James above Newport News in 1625 is difficult to determine. There had been a number of land patents issued prior to this date. One for 100 acres, on August 14, 1624, was to Edward Waters at "Blunt point" and several others were issued four months later in the area between the point and Newport News. Some were to old residents of Newport News and Kecoughtan and several were issued to new arrivals. One grant for 150 acres to Maurice Thompson had been made as early as March 4, 1621. Patented acreage at "Blunt Pointe" and "belowe Blunt Point" in 1625 embraced some 2,200 acres and 1,390 acres respectively.

The massacre of 1622 forced the withdrawal of any who may have been located in the area at that date. Included in the list of those killed at the time was Edward Walters, his wife, child, maid and boy all at "Master Edward Walters his house" which may have been in the Blunt Point vicinity. If this were really Edward Waters who received the patent at Blunt Point in 1624, it would mean that he had already established himself here. Such is conceivable since, at the time of the massacre, he and his wife were made prisoners by the Nansemond Indians and possibly could have been listed as dead. He was fortunate in being able to manage an escape and took refuge at Elizabeth City (Kecoughtan).

Waters was an ancient planter who had come to Virginia with Gates, reaching the Colony in 1610. He was one of a party who returned to Bermuda for hogs for Virginia. Circumstances intervened and he remained there about seven years. It was not until about 1617 that he returned to Virginia where he was married and settled down. In 1625 he was listed as living at Elizabeth City with his wife, son and daughter, "borne in Virginia." His muster then included six servants and five others.

In a statement made by a number of Virginia planters on April 30, 1623, there is mention of the plantation at "Blunt point" which would imply an established settlement here at that time. It was enumerated along with a number of others, including Newport News, which were described "as verie fruitfull and pleasant seates." This was ten months after Captain Samuel Each's offer to "erect before the end of March [1623] uppon the oyster bankes, a block-house, that should forbid the passage of any shipp" up the James. Each felt that he could lay his vessel near "Blunt point" and do this with dispatch with his mariners and twelve carpenters. The Governor and Council embraced his offer to build this "Block house about Blunt Point." Company officials in England, too, liked the idea very much. Seemingly, however, it never materialized. Instead, talk turned to the fort which was undertaken at Warrascoyack on the opposite shore of the James.

Mulberry Island (43)

On the north side of the James River some ten miles below Jamestown, this "island" embraces some ten square miles of ground. Its name evidently was derived from a heavy growth of the native Virginia mulberry trees (*Morus rubra*). This must have been the case since "Mulberry Island" and "Mulberry Point" were in use as place designations as early as July, 1610. It was so named even before it was settled.

When Gates was proceeding down river, having abandoned Jamestown, in June, 1610, it was just off Mulberry Island that he encountered Lord De La Warr's "long boat" which gave word of reinforcements and supplies. This saved the Colony and Gates reversed his course and returned to Jamestown. In this way Mulberry Island is linked with this decisive meeting which greatly affected the survival of the Colony.

It is not clear when actual settlement of the Island began. Seemingly it was not before 1617 or 1618. In any event, about this time, settlers did begin to drift in to this section of the James River basin. In 1619 it appears that Captain William Pierce patented 650 acres in this quarter. Pierce had been in Virginia since 1610 and in 1617 was well established being Captain of the Guard at Jamestown where he had "the fairest [house] in all Virginia." Now, however, he removed to his new holding where, before March, 1622, he built another home and established his residence.

Another prominent patentee at Mulberry Island was John Rolfe who had "land on Mulberry Island Virginia" before March 10, 1621. He and "some others," including William Pierce, obtained 1,700 acres by patent and proceeded to "plant" it. His chief residence at the time was in Bermuda Hundred and it is doubtful that he resided here. He had, it might be mentioned, in 1620, married Jane the daughter of Captain William Pierce and he appears to have lost his life in the Indian massacre.

It is not known how many others "planted," or lived, here at this time. Evidently it was not sufficient to send a representative to the Assembly in 1619. Whatever growth it enjoyed was checked by the Indian massacre in 1622. It is recorded that Thomas Pierce, probably a son of William, his wife and child, two men and "a French boy," were killed at Thomas' house "over against Mulberry Island." The resettlement of the area after the massacre was delayed. No persons are listed from this locality in 1624 nor were there representatives in the Assembly of the same year. Within a year, however, the picture had changed.

The census of January, 1625 lists thirty persons, twenty-five males and five women, at "Mulburie Island." Not much else is listed in the muster except the arms of the settlement. The twenty-two suits of armor, the thirty-seven "fixed pieces" and the forty-two swords would indicate that protection was uppermost in the plans. There were several distinct musters including those of Anthony Baram and Thomas Harwood, yet the largest was that of Captain William Pierce. Although not in residence himself, he had thirteen servants at Mulberry Island. Except for Pierce's, there were no other servants save one of Thomas Harwood.

Martin's Hundred (44)

This was one of the earliest of the "particular" plantations and had a larger and more vigorous life than most. It has been said that this might be listed as the leading, or model, Hundred in the Colony. It was one organized and promoted by a group within, yet outside of, the regular Company projects. It was named for Richard Martin, an attorney for the London Company. He was a leading member in the Society of Martin's Hundred as this special group of adventurers was known. Another leader in the sponsoring group was Sir John Wolstenholme whose name was associated with the town, described in January, 1622 as "the Towne in Martin's Hundred [which] is now seated called Wolstenholme Towne."

Wolstenholme was located on the James, it seems, and the boundaries of the Hundred, when laid down in 1621, were measured five miles along the "river called (Kinge) James River" in each direction from it. This was five miles toward Jamestown and five toward "Newportes Newes." Northward the bound was the Queenes River alias Pacomunky [York]." It is of interest to note that the boundaries were to "the middest" of the rivers. Roughly its 80,000 acres lay on the north side of the James between Archer's Hope and Mulberry Island.

In October, 1618, the Society sent its first colonists to Virginia. These made up a party of 280 who reached Virginia several months later in the *Guift of God*. Several additional groups were sent out in 1619, a large party in 1620 and others in 1621. The latter were sent, it was recorded, "to plante and inhabite and to erect and make perfect a church and towne there already begunne." At the time of the Assembly in 1619 it was an established community and sent its representatives up to Jamestown—John Boys and John Jackson.

It appears to have been a determined lot of "ancient adventurers" who sponsored Martin's Hundred and the record indicates that they worked hard and zealously to make it a paying organization. They were, however, often beset with difficulties. Shipmasters and mariners abused them as did the "Capemarchant," according to their reports. When they sought Company shares to sustain losses in one shipment to Virginia, Sir Edwin Sandys reminded them that they were a particular group. He related "As Martins Hundred hath been at great charges, so have divers other hundreds, so have also beene many perticuler persons, Captaine Bargrave alone hath brought and sett out divers shipps . . . Sir Thomas Gates, and Sir Thomas Dale, besides a multitude of other[s], who have spent a large portion of their estates therein. . . ."

In May, 1621, Yeardley wrote concerning the arrival of servants to be located at Martin's Hundred. He described the difficulty of making land assignments "because we have never a surveyour in the lande." He added too that "the undertakers at Martins Hundred would thinke themselves muche wronged, if any other should be sett on worke to divide their groundes." He commented, too, that a proper division might be better since he had heard that the Society "intende . . . to buy out the Indians of Chischiack [on the York River]."

Martin's Hundred suffered severely in the massacre of 1622. The slaughter took a total of seventy-eight persons including the commander. Among those killed were a score of women and children showing that family life was well developed here. The loss was so great that the settlement was temporarily abandoned along with a great many others in Virginia. The abandonment was of

105

short duration, it seems, for new references soon appear such as that naming Captain Ralph Hamor "to have absolute power, and comand in all matters of war over all the people of Martins Hundred." In any case "the replantinge" was left to the Society which had originally established it. Although the Company deemed it, along with others which had been deserted, "of absolute necessitie," it was too busy with its own projects to aid materially.

The Society "set forth a verie chargeable supply of people" in October, 1622. When William Harwood was mentioned for the Council, Martin's Hundred asked that he not be named since they needed his services full time. Reverend Robert Paulett was named instead. In April, 1623 it was a going concern although life was dark in the eyes of Richard Frethorne who wrote of the danger, hunger, and the heavy work. He related "ther is indeed some foule [fowle], but wee are not allowed to goe, and get it, but must worke hard both earlie, and late for a messe of water gruell, and a mouthfull of bread, and beife." He stated that of twenty who came the last year but three were left. In all, he said, "wee are but thirty-two." The Indians he feared; "the nighest helpe that Wee have is ten miles of us." Here "wee lye even in their teeth." The break in the monotony, it seems, was an occasional trip to Jamestown "that is ten miles of us, there be all the ships that come to the land, and there must deliver their goodes." The trip up took from noon till night on the tide. The return was the same.

Nothing came, at this time, of the proposal for "runninge a pale from Martin's Hundred to Cheskacke," between the York and the James rivers. The stockade across the peninsula was still a decade away. When built it would be several miles to the west. There is nothing to indicate that the church, or school, for which William Whitehead left funds in his will in 1623, ever materialized. The plan was that it be built in Martin's Hundred.

Evidently conditions at this time were at a low ebb. George Sandys felt it was a pity that the project could not be pushed more vigorously. When the plantation was asked to take a number of the "infidelles children to be brought up" the officials asked to be excused since they were "sorely weakened and . . . in much confusion." The Indians, too, were still around. The Governor in May, 1623 urged that the "Commander" keep watch, insure the carrying of arms and prevent stragglers from loitering about. The Indians were suspected of coming to "spy and observe." Seemingly the plantation, perhaps already a parish in the church organization, was not represented in the Assembly in 1624.

At this time Martin's Hundred was reported to have twenty-three persons, but twenty-eight had died within the year, two being killed. At the time of the general census of the next year, there were but thirty-one, a fact that indicates small growth. To accommodate these there were seven houses, supplies of corn and fish and some cattle and hogs. The settlement was well stocked in weapons with thirty-two armors of various types, thirty-one swords, and fifty-two small arms. Perhaps William Harwood, who was in charge, remembered well the massacre.

ARCHER'S HOPE (45)

The place name Archer's Hope is older even than Jamestown located several miles upstream from it. Here on May 12, 1607 colonists went ashore to evaluate a spot as a site for their initial settlement. It had advantages, yet it was not possible to bring the ships in close to the shore so the next day they made choice of Jamestown. Gabriel Archer, it appears, liked the spot and it was named in his honor. The site was at the mouth of College (Archer's Hope) Creek, the waterway that may have been used by the Spanish Jesuit missionaries four decades earlier when, in 1570, they were searching for a mission site in Virginia.

Even though the settlers elected not to establish themselves here in 1607, it was in the Jamestown neighborhood and very likely was soon in use. It is clearly established that a distinct community took form within a dozen years. Unfortunately not much is known prior to 1619 when a number of land grants were made to men like William Fairfax, John Fowler, William Capp and Joakim Andrews, most with established Jamestown connections. It was at Archer's Hope that the great massacre reached closest to Jamestown. Five persons were slain "At Ensigne Spence his house." Following the slaughter the settlement appears to have been abandoned with survivors taking refuge elsewhere, perhaps, at Jamestown.

The abandonment was of short duration. On February 16, 1624 some fourteen persons were in residence here, at least three family units and presumably a number of servants. Evidently this was not sufficient to merit representation in the Assembly of 1624. The fact that Archer's Hope had a commander, Thomas Bransby, and that its inhabitants had been cautioned not to go too far from their homes alone, even when armed, leads to the conclusion that there was still danger from the Indian, "the Enemie," even in 1625. At the same time there is evidence of an expanding agriculture and increasing population. Archer's Hope had its disturbers of the peace as well in citizens such as Joseph Johnson who from time to time found himself answering to the General Court.

The census of 1625 named fourteen persons as constituting the settlement of Archer's Hope which then extended to the east as well as to the west of the creek bearing the same name. Each of the four major entries showed a single house although there must have been more than this in aggregate. On a population basis the amount of arms and armor available would indicate that, perhaps, the community had a military cast. Food supplies were about normal, yet no livestock is shown except eight hogs which included "piggs" as well.

Altogether, by this date, at least 3,000 acres of land had been taken up by fifteen persons, many of them "ancient planters." The largest grant, 750 acres, had been to Rev. Richard Buck, minister for Jamestown. Richard Kingsmill had received 300 acres as had Ensign William Spence and John Fowler. Two, William Claiborne and John Jefferson, had 250 acre parcels, but all others had lesser amounts. Only three were shown as "planted." The list omits a grant of some size to George Sandys which was located in the precincts of Archer's Hope but well to the east "on the ponds, dividing from the land of Martin's Hundred." On the west Archer's Hope was separated from James City's "Neck-of-Land" by the Jamestown parish glebe land.

"Neck-of-Land neare James Citty" (46)

This area lay behind Jamestown Island on the mainland between Mill and Powhatan Creeks. Even though separated from "James Citty" only by the narrow Back River and its marshes, settlement seemingly was delayed for a decade. At least the records are silent on the matter if colonists did establish here in the first years.

It clearly emerges as an established settlement in 1624 when its population was given at twenty-five persons including at least four families with servants and dependents. That same year it sent its own burgess to the Assembly at Jamestown, its most prominent resident, Richard Kingsmill. Early in 1625 the population stood at eighteen, six freemen, three women, three children, five servants and a single negro. A comparison of the names given in 1624 with those in 1625 points up the shifting of persons that must have been a part of the Virginia scene at this time. As might be expected from its proximity, a number of the residents of the "Neck-of-Land" had property also at Jamestown or in the Island.

The 1625 muster listings included six houses, a boat, twenty-six and a half barrels of corn as well as some "flesh," fish, and meal. Livestock embraced eleven cattle and thirty-one hogs, "yong & old." There was only one "armour" and two "coats of male" yet small arms, shot and powder were in greater supply. The General Court records offer an occasional glimpse of life here in these years. There was, for example, the decision in 1624 that the "lands and goods" of John Phillmore, who died without a will, should be given to Elizabeth Pierce "unto whom he was assured and ment to have maryed."

This then was the Virginia of 1625—a settled area embracing the James River basin and the lower part of the Eastern Shore. It was very rural with the people busy about the task of developing a new land. Some twenty-seven distinct communities, groups, or settlements were enumerated at this time, yet even these may not fully suggest the scope of the occupied, or cultivated, land. These settlements were chiefly along the north and south shores of the James River, eastward from the falls to the Chesapeake Bay. Though loosely knit geographically, they were a unit politically with affairs, for the most part, administered from the capital "citty" of Jamestown. Actually the Colony even now was poised for an extension of its frontier inland from the river fringe especially across to the banks of the York and into what was to become the Norfolk area. This would precede "the push to the west" that later became such a familiar pattern.

In the first seventeen years, despite hardship, suffering, death, discouragement and defeats, a great deal had been accomplished in Virginia. The colonists, some of whom had already become "ancient planters," had met and learned many of the ways of the wilderness and the new environment. They had learned to survive and had gained knowledge of the country's advantages and disadvantages and its nature and extent. After many false starts, a source of wealth had been found in tobacco. Security was coming to replace insecurity and individual well-being was rising above the earlier general storehouse or magazine system. Government, too, after several changes of direction, had become stable and even embraced a representative legislative assembly.

110

It seems that King James I, when he took over, directly, the management of the Colony, must have found that the Virginia Company of London had built well in the New World. Otherwise, the change of administration would have been more disrupting than it was in Virginia.

SELECTED READINGS

Andrews, Charles M., *The Colonial Period of American History: The Settlements I*. New Haven, c.1934 (several printings).

Andrews, Matthew Page, *Virginia: The Old Dominion*. New York, c.1937.

Brown, Alexander, *The First Republic in America*. Boston, 1898.

Brown, Alexander (ed.), *The Genesis of the United States*. . . . Boston, 1896. 2 volumes.

Chandler, J. A. C., and Thames, T. B., *Colonial Virginia*. Richmond, 1907.

Craven, Wesley Frank, *The Dissolution of the Virginia Company of London*. New York, 1932.

Forman, Henry Chandlee, *Jamestown and St. Mary's: Buried Cities of Romance*. Baltimore, 1938.

Hamor, Ralph, *A True Discourse of the Present Estate of Virginia and the Successe of the Affaires There Till the 18 of June, 1614*. London, 1615. The J. Munsell reprint (Albany, 1860) The Virginia State Library are more readily available.

McIlwaine, H. R. (ed.), *Minutes of the Council and General Court of Virginia, 1622-1632, 1670-1676*. Richmond, 1924.

Neill, Edward D., *History of the Virginia Company of London*. Albany, New York, 1869.

Virginia Vetusta, During the Reign of James the First. . . . Albany, New York, 1885.

Powell, William S., "Books in the Virginia Colony before 1624." *The William and Mary Quarterly*, 3rd Series, V, 177-184 (April, 1948).

Rolfe, John, *A True Relation of Virginia* [in 1616] as printed by Henry C. Taylor. New Haven, 1951.

Sams, Conway Whittle, *The Conquest of Virginia*. 4 volumes ("The Forest Primeval," "The First Attempt," "The Second Attempt," and "The Third Attempt"). New York, 1916-1939.

Smith, John, *The Travels and Works of Captain John Smith*. Edited by Edward Arber with introduction. Edinburgh, 1910. 2 volumes.

Stanard, Mary Newton, *The Story of Virginia's First Century*. Philadelphia, 1928.

Strachey, William, *The Historie of Travell into Virginia Britania (1612)*. Edited by Louis B. Wright and Virginia Freund and printed for the

Hakluyt Society. London, 1953. (Also available in an edition edited by H.H. Major. London, 1849.)

Tyler, Lyon Gardiner (ed.), *Narratives of Early Virginia, 1606-1625.* New York, 1930.

The Cradle of the Republic: Jamestown and James River. Richmond, Va., 1906 (2nd edition).

Virginia Company, *The Records of the Virginia Company of London.* Edited by Susan Myra Kingsbury. Washington, D. C., 1906-1935. 4 volumes.

Wertenbaker, Thomas Jefferson, *The First Americans 1607-1690. A History of American Life,* Volume II. New York, c.1927 (various printings).

Wingfield, Edward Maria, *A Discourse of Virginia.* Edited by Charles Deane. Boston, 1860.

Wright, Louis B., *Atlantic Frontier: Colonial American Civilization: 1607-1761.* New York, 1947.

Yonge, Samuel H., *The Site of Old "James Towne" 1607-1698.* Richmond, c.1907 (several reprints).

APPENDIX

Supplies for Virginia

One of the most informative ways, perhaps, to get an idea of daily living in early Virginia is to read, and study, a list of the household, personal and general objects which were sent to the Colony. One of the most detailed such lists that has been preserved is one that itemizes the cargo sent in the ship, *Supply*, which left England in September, 1620, bound for Berkeley Hundred. This is given in digest below. It is adapted from the list in the Smith of Nibley Papers and is available in published form in the *Bulletin of the New York Public Library*, III, No. 7 (July, 1899), pp. 283-290 as well as in the *Records of the Virginia Company of London*, III, pp. 385-393.

Bought at London

15 grosse of buttons; 60 eles of linnen cloth; 15 eles of canvas; 10 yards of blue linnen for facinge the doublets; tape and thread; 42 yards of brode cloth at 6s the yard for 20 cassacks & breeches; 57 yards of dyed holmes fustian at 18d the yard for 20 doublets; makinge the said 20 doublets cassacks & breeches at 3s 4d; 10 doublets & breeches of russet lether with lether lynings £8 15s & 9 gros of lether buttons 10s In the wholl with the makynge; glas beades of severall sorts; drugs & phisicks bought of Mr Barton Apothecary by doctor Gulsons direccon for the flipp & scurvy &c; wainscot boxe and hay to pack the same in &c; drifatt to send downe the 30 sutes of apparell and cariage of the same from the Taylors to the wayne at Holborne bridge & porters.

Bought at Stoke

20 bushells of wheat at 3s 6d; 336 lbs. of butter at 5d; 336 lbs. of cheese at 25s the 112 lbs.; 2 corslets & 2 callivers furnished; a musket.

Bought at Nibley and in the Country.

22 bushells of white pease bought by Mr Smyth of Mris. Leigh of Combe at 2s the bushell 44s & cariage to Nibley 2s 6d; 9 bushells more of white pease bought of Sam Trotman at 22s the bushell (which were the best of all.); 9 bushells of 3 square wheat in ears in 2 great pipes at 4s; 12 bushells & halfe of malt (dryed on purpose) put into another great

114

canary pipe at 2s; 3 pipes, & for one other pipe, 2 hoggsheads &, 2 lesser casks to put the said pease in, & caryage in 2 waynes from Nibley to Berkeley, with 12s spent by the plowman there, & to the couper to head & dresse them.

Bought at Bristoll faire and after there.

522 dozen of buttons, parte thread, parte haire and 6 dozen of greene silke; 12 dozen yards of garteringe, of 2 sorts & 4 colors &c; 6 grosse of poynts beinge 72 dozen whereof the one half of lether, the other of thread; 5 paire of double boxcombes & 6 bone combs; 10 dozen of knives whereof 9 dozen of one sort and one dozen of another sort; one dozen of sisers; one dozen of womens sheares; 4 payres of Taylors sheares of 2 sorts; one dozen of paringe knives; 6 other knives; 600 & an halfe of cheese bought by Wm Hopton at 14s & 16s the hundred beinge 101 cheeses; 4 quires & an halfe of paper for all the servants indentures and other draughts, ec; 54 ells of dowlas at 15d ob. for shirts; 58 els 3 quarters of canvas for sheets at 14d; 24 els of canvas at 15d and 66 els of canvas at 13d ob; 52 els of canvas at 15 for shirts; 84 ells of canvas at 13d for sheets; 81 ells quarter of canvas at 14d; 82 ells and an halfe at 14d of canvas; 56 ells & an halfe of canvas at 14d; 32 ells of dowlas at 14d; 3 dozen of fallinge bands at 7s 6d the dozen; 5 dozen of fallinge bands at 6s 6d the dozen; 2 dozen falling bands at 5s 6d the dozen; 10 dozen of handkercheifs; 49 payre of Irish stockins; 22 payre of Irish stockins; 34 payre of Irish stockins; one barrell of tarre; one barrell of pitch; 6 hoggsheads of baysalt for Virginia; 30 stone of stocks at 2s 6; 10 reaphooks; 2 fryinge pans; 2 bolts of browne thread; one bolt of black thread; 8 lbs. browne thread; 20 pick axes; 40 weedinge howes; 30 spades; 2 sithes; 10 felling axes; 6 squaring axes; 20 bed mats; 10 bushells di. [i.e. one-half] peck of oatmeale at 4s; 5 bushells of oatmeal grots at 6s; 2 grindstones; 2 french mill stones; 102 lbs. of sope; 10 traces of onyons; 10 gallons 3 quarts of oyle & the runlet to put it in; 6 baskets used about the ship; 6 bells; 6 bandeleres; 1 quarter of 100 of match; 6 swords; makinge 51 shirts at 3d & 2 towells; makinge 25 payre of sheets; 100 di & 13 lbs. of lead beinge 6 bars; 200 of lead shot at 1d the lb.; 160 lbs. di of powder at 15d; a little caske to put 12 lbs. of powder in; 200 payre of shoes of 4 sizes.

Garden seeds vzt parsnip, carret, cabbage, turnep, lettuice, onyon mustared and garlick; 2 tun of sider bought at Bristoll; 1 hoggeshead of new sider sent Mr Thorpe; hallinge to the storehouse and lynes to maile in it; charges of Robt Lawford at Bristoll imployed divers dayes buyinge of provisions &c; 60 gallons & one pottle of aqua vite at 3s; 22500 nayles of severall sorts; 2000 of hobnayles; 4000 of sparrowbills; bags to put nayles in and to the porter; given to the poore and spent at hiringe the first ship by Felgate; given to break of from that ships after 14 days; one dryfatt and 3 tun of caske untrimd; 15 dozen of candles at 4s 4d the dozen; 2

115

barrells of Irish beoffe bought by Toby Felgate; one other barrell bought by Tho. Kewis; 2142 lbs. of beoffe & porke, salt for it & charges in saltinge and barrellinge beinge in 13 barrells; 200 di [i.e. one-half, or 50 lbs.] of codfish at 46s the 100 called Cornish fish; cariage of 1300 waight from London parte by horse & parte by wayne to Bristoll & waighinge; a chest to put small parcells in; 100 3 quarters 7 lb. of iron hoopes to hoope 6 tun of beere at 3d the pound; dyet & lodginge in Bristoll upon one accompt at the Horshooe and Horsmeat & hire of Toby Felgates horse twice to Nibley.

Markams works of husbandry & huswifry bound togeather and for the like of Gowges &c; the copies of the counsells order for fishinge & about tobacco and of Sir Edwin Sandis project, and of the artificiall wine, to be sent over to Mr Thorpe, payd the Secretary; 18 tun of beere at 36s p. tun and for 3 barrells spent in the ship; 8800 of bisket at 12s the 100 lbs. and 21 lbs. over and a quarter of 100 more; 20 ruggs at 8s the peece; 100 of monmoth caps and bands; a boylinge kettle filled for the ship at 17d the lb. beinge 36 lbs. di [i.e. one-half]; 60 gallons of sack at 2s 6d the gallon in 4 runlets; one hoggeshed of wine vinegar; cloutleather 32d shoothread 26 dozen 4s and 4 half quarter of hemp 4s 1d; to the couper upon his bill for 39 tun of caske and 2 barrells of all the fraight contayninge 142 vessels bought of him besides what came from Mr Tracy & Mr Smyth; and to the coupers journeyman for many labors by him done; to Mr Ewens in parte of the wages for the hire of his ship before hand by acquitance and by indorsement of his chartre party; to the grosser for sugar, pepper, ginger, cynamon, nutmegs, cloves, mace, dates, raisons, currants damaske prunes, rice, saffron, almonds, brimston, starch & one ream of paper; a masons great hammer & trouell bought by Richard Piers for himselfe; 8 bushells of meale at 4s the bushell; 2 great & 2 lesser lanthornes 5s 2 shod shovels, 20d bellowes, lables, trenches, mustard bolls, tape cannells, bread baskets, wooden spoones, tundish, 18 cans, mustard pot, 12 porridge dishes 18 quarter cans, 2 horne tunnels, 2 horne cups, a pair of scales, 3 little drynking cups, 3 dozen wodden sawcers, 4 dozen platters, 6 wyre candlesticks, 2 panyars, & 1 pepercorne all wood; makinge of bolsters and other parcells upon many particulars, as hallyers, 29s 10d wood 23s 4d cordage to trusse and cabynes 7s 4d padlockes 4s 6d, 3 spades & 2 howes 9d makinge 30 sheets and 21 shirts, 11s 8d 28 bolsters makinge &c.

Bought of Mr Tracy.

100 payre of knit stockins; watchinge the wayne & cariage of the 13 brode clothes that Benedict Webbe sent to Bristoll to the storehouse; 9 swordes; 9 corslets; 9 muskers wherof 6 are with snaphanses; 6 callivers; 4 coates of plate; 4 partizans; 12 felling axes made in Deane, and for 2 squaring axes; 10 hatchets; 24 augurs of severall sorts; 2 handsawes; 12

sithes; 24 reaphooks; a vise for a smyth; a bras serine for a glister pipe; 15 peeces beoffe roafed [?] & 4 tongues; 43 lb. of cheese; 9 flitches of bacon; 20 bushells of white pease at 2s 4d; a barrell of pippen vinegar; 2 broad-axes; 2 felling axes; 2 adizes; 2 handsawes; 2 hatchets; one 2 inch augur; 6 turnynge tools; 2 googes; 4 brode chesills; 7 playnge irons; small chesills; one twibill; mendinge of servants tooles; 4 millpecks; one anvill; 2 turn-inge irons; 13 brode clothes of 29 yards the peece and 7 brode bought of Benedict Webb by Mr Tracy; buckerom & canvas to pack them in; to Boswell the apothecary upon his bill for drugs and other like stuffs bought by Mr. Pawlet as appeareth.

Payd Mr Felgate upon accompt for charges about the breadroome, & cabins, for joyners worke, pitche, náyles, bordes &c; payd for wages of 5 of our seamen for 3 weeks di [i.e. one-half] 4s the weeke dayly helpinge ended 17 September Saturday night; and for the dyet of Toby Felgate at Bristol for 7 weeks at 6s p. weeke; payd Toby Felgate upon his bill for the charges of himselfe and hire of his horse to Bristoll and cariage of his sea cards, affaires & apparell; payd at the Horshooe for a chamber to stowe our goods bought at St James faire for 5 weeks; imprest to Mr Felgate to buy 1000 couple of Newfoundland fish; 2 sives to make gunpowder in Virginia; a barre of iron and hangers in the cookroome in the ship; the hire of the Swanne cellar 5s and for Hendens cellar for all our goods 11s; charges of diet of Mr Smyth & parte of the company at the White Lyon, and for the bord wages of other parte of the company for 14 dayes as by accompt kept by Willm Archard; paper, inke & parchment for com-issions and quadripartite covenants & indentures &c; 2 boxes for cariage of comissions, lettres indentures &c into Virginia; the hire of a boat that caryed Mris Tracy & the weomen & children from Bristoll to Crockhampill; to the boatmen at Barkley for caryage of 2 tun di of pease, wheat, wheat eares malt &c to Bristoll; to Mr Willet Customer outwards for the customs of 10 brode clothes & pretermitted dutyes, which is to be repayd upon cer-tificate from Sir Garroway & Sir John Worsuam; payd Mr. Tracys bill for a tramell net; payd for the passage of 20 men & weomen from the partes of Hayles to Bristoll, & the hire of some horses dyet & lodginge at the Horshooe and at Mris Lewis house and lodginge of many servants as by severall bills appeareth over & besides what Mr Smyth thought in-differently fit to abate which Mr Tracy referred to him &c; for wrytinge & ingrossinge the 2 comissions quadripartite covenants 35 payre of in-dentures and divers other particulars; sent to Mr Tracy upon his lettres after I was come to Nibley to be supplyed, whilst he lay for wynd at Crockampill with all his company &c.

This list makes it crystal clear that supplying Virginia was both a costly and time consuming operation. It is clear, too, that supplies were of the nature that encouraged permanent colonization and residence in Virginia. Those Englishmen who founded the Colony took as much of the English way of life with them as was possible be it personal or political rights and freedom, books, food, clothing, utensils, or working tools.